As Karl Barth saw him:

Calvin is a cataract, a primeval forest, a demonic power, something directly down from the Himalaya, absolutely Chinese, strange, mythological; I lack completely the means, the suction cups, even to assimilate this phenomenon, not to speak of presenting it adequately. . . . I could gladly and profitably set myself down and spend the rest of my life just with Calvin.

Karl Barth, to Eduard Thurneysen, June 8, 1922

As a contemporary historian saw him:

Calvin invented a new kind of man in Geneva — Reformation man — and in him sketched out what was to become modern civilization.

Émile G. Léonard, *Histoire générale du Protestantisme*

As the translator of the Institutes *saw him:*

Calvinism is a disease, the only cure for which is further doses of itself.

Ford Lewis Battles

LIGHT FOR THE CITY

Calvin's Preaching, Source of Life and Liberty

Lester De Koster

WILLIAM B. EERDMANS PUBLISHING COMPANY
GRAND RAPIDS, MICHIGAN / CAMBRIDGE, U.K.

© 2004 Wm. B. Eerdmans Publishing Co.

Wm. B. Eerdmans Publishing Co.
255 Jefferson Ave. S.E., Grand Rapids, Michigan 49503 /
P.O. Box 163, Cambridge CB3 9PU U.K.
www.eerdmans.com

Printed in the United States of America

09 08 07 06 05 04   7 6 5 4 3 2 1

Library of Congress Cataloging-in-Publication Data

De Koster, Lester, 1915-
    Light for the city: Calvin's preaching, source of life and liberty / Lester De Koster.
        p.   cm.
    Includes bibliographical references.
    ISBN 0-8028-2780-2 (pbk.)
        1. Calvin, Jean, 1509-1564.   2. Predestination — Sermons —History and
criticism.   3. Kingdom of God — History of doctrines — 16th century.
4. Geneva (Switzerland) — Church history — 16th century.   I. Title.

BT809.D45   2004
230'.42'092 — dc22

                                                    2004046984

Excerpts from Calvin's *Institutes* are reproduced from John Calvin, *Institutes of the Christian Religion* (Library of Christian Classics), edited by John T. McNeill. Used by permission of Westminster John Knox Press.

Unless noted otherwise, the Scripture quotations in this publication are from the Revised Standard Version of the Bible, copyrighted 1946, 1952 © 1971, 1973 by the Division of Christian Education of the National Council of Churches of Christ in the U.S.A., and from the New Revised Standard Version Bible, copyright © 1989 by the Division of Christian Education of the National Council of Churches of Christ in the U.S.A., and quotations from both sources are used by permission.

To Ruth

Without Her, Nothing

Contents

In Appreciation

One is recipient, over half a decade's tussling with a manuscript, of a variety of kindly considerations generously aimed at its enrichment. To each such donor, a hearty thanks; especially to Eerdmans' Managing Editor Linda Bieze, herself as personally pleasant as professionally competent.

LDK

Forewarning

It's nice, even profitable, to know where authors think they are going.

Makes it easier to decide whether or not you want to tag along.

The thesis of this slight tribute can be simply put.

We know that Christianity is a multi-faceted thing. Only God knows in how many ways his Spirit enriches the world. Calvin/Calvinism is one of them.

And how is that?

Calvin enrolls his *Institutes of the Christian Religion* among the world's great books with its opening sentences: "Nearly all the wisdom we possess, that is to say true and sound wisdom, consists in two parts: the knowledge of God and of ourselves. But, while joined by many bonds, which one precedes and brings forth the other is not easy to discern" (*Institutes*, I,1,1).

For him, Christianity comes to focus upon Wisdom. He has in mind, and intent, the "wisdom" God provides for the well-being of his Image-bearing humankind. The wisdom comes by way of the divine Word incarnate in Holy Scripture. The capacity to hear and seek to do that wisdom is provided by the vicarious self-sacrifice of the Son of God in Jesus Christ upon Calvary. The Church is called into being in response to the Lord's command to "make disciples" by "teaching them to observe all that I have commanded you" (Matt. 28:19-20), that is, teaching all who believe to incarnate the revealed wisdom of their Maker in their behavior.

The "wisdom" that Calvin has in view informs daily rosaries of hours strung in living obedience to the revealed will of the living God, along the common paths of daily life. The accumulation of such obedient behavior, as led by the obedient pulpit, combines to realize the civilized vision of the City, ancient dream of the "brightest and the best" of the genius visited by God upon his children through his Word.

Liberated by the reality of divine predestination (we will get to that later) from the Lutheran absorption in "salvation by faith," and from the Catholic commitment to Church-defined "good works," Calvin can boldly say (to Catholic Cardinal Sadoleto):

"It is not a very sound theology to confine a man's thoughts so much to himself, and not to set before him, as the prime motive of his existence, zeal to illustrate the glory of God. For we are born first of all for God, and not for ourselves. . . . This zeal ought to exceed all thought and care for our own advantage. . . . It certainly is the part of the Christian man to ascend higher than merely to seek and secure the salvation of his own soul" (*Reformation Debate*, 58).

"Merely" the soul? Yes, so he said. And "higher" than soul-salvation? His word, too. *Higher!* **To build, say, community called "city"?!**

Preached from off the pulpits for which the Church is divinely made and sustained, God's biblical Word takes incarnation in human selves and behavior, creating the community long known in the West as the City. Calvinist pulpits implanted the Word even now flourishing in the great democratic achievements of the Western world.

That's Calvinism.

We can try here, incidentally, to amend an oversight and abort an error. It is the oversight which distances the modern mind from one of its own sparkling springs of social and political democracy, the thought and work of Calvin. It is the error which chooses by deprecation of the Bible to divorce the modern world from the dynamic found only in the living Word of the living God.

No . . . Calvin was not the tyrant of Geneva so popular in school texts and media asides. Quite to the contrary, Calvin/Calvinism facilitated the aim of the inspired Word of God to give historical form to the

Western democratic mind and waits now to provide the desperately desirable antidote to the foolish and oxymoronic cliché of *"separation* of Church and state" through emphasis upon the revealed truth that Church and state, private and public life, personal and societal behavior are all fused under the one Word of God and cannot be *separated.*

German historian Oswald Spengler says in his exquisitely phrased *Decline of the West,* "While the Lutheran movement advanced leaderless in central Europe, Calvin viewed his rule in Geneva as the starting-point of a systematic subjugation of the world under a Protestantism unfalteringly thought out to its logical conclusion. Therefore he, and he alone, became a world-power . . ." (II: 299).

The result is described by Michael Walzer: "Luther in his old age was a provincial figure and a political conservative; Calvin in his last years was an international figure and, some would have said, the inexhaustible source of sedition and rebellion" (23). Marxist genius Leon Trotsky, who with Lenin carved the Soviet Union out of the Russian Revolution of 1917, caught that, saying that Marx and Calvin were the two most revolutionary figures in Western history. Could that be said of Calvinist pulpits now?

If closer acquaintance with this "world power," his gifts, and his influence could interest — and perhaps even profit — you, might we walk along a bit together?

It doesn't look to be too long a journey.

Preface

At first encounter, Karl Barth's puzzling characterization of Calvin, quoted as an epigraph to this book, seems at best an exaggerated reaction to an intensive immersion in Calvin's literary heritage — *Institutes*, sermons, letters, treatises. For Barth that was in preparation in 1922 for a course of insightful lectures recently published in English by Eerdmans as *The Theology of John Calvin*.

Calvin had not been, Barth says somewhere, high on the totem pole of academic preference in his student days. Barth must master him solo. The translator, Geoffrey Bromiley, speaks of the lectures as "the struggling of one giant with another." But who, including Barth himself, has been able to flesh out, tempting as it would be to try, *his* Calvin (this one):

> "... a cataract, a primeval forest, a demonic power, something directly down from the Himalaya, absolutely Chinese, strange, mythological ..." (Smart, 101).

Written as between close friends. But don't just toss that off! My experience has been, over some decades, that on growing acquaintance, Calvin more and more validates Barth's expostulation. God chose him to be a knight-errant of his Word, it now seems to me, a kind of pre-Quixote who, though thinking himself timid, dauntlessly rode the Scripture as his Rocsinante into the faces of the Adversary everywhere, thus to open the world of the West to the democratic — meaning potentially *everyone's* — experience of the freedom of God. That is, a freedom born of Word-discipline.

Much beset was Calvin in his time, all along the way, by the minions of the demonic. Model was he, too, for determined identification of that Adversary in every enmity encountered by humankind. For him, "flesh and blood" only front for his Satanic majesty, who lurks in the shadows from whence arise spiritual clashes everyday, everywhere. Calvin's weapon was the sword of the Word, drawn from the scabbard of Scripture and brandished upon the obedient pulpit; the enemy was ever the Devil; the victory was emergence of the democratic world, so far from perfection yet so close to the legendary City of ancient aspiration.

Yes, such a Calvin indeed there was, but how might he be grasped as well as experienced?!

As one's acquaintance with this Calvin deepens and expands and his dimensions merge into the inscrutable on more and more fronts, it does appear that only one as gifted as a Barth could crystallize him in words that come strikingly to evoke the mystique of his being. He was, in the way Barth presumably intended, cataract, strange, mythological, demonic — all as described, and just so being a divinely chosen channel into modernity. He eludes systematization. He became "Uncle John" here at my home, rather long ago, over the decade during which our family of six endured my grinding out a thesis on his "living" ideas. He is still just "Uncle." I claim only to be an appreciative idolater.

Maybe Barth's language is a lens useful for sensing best what it was about him that motivated Spengler's estimate.

Terms: "City" and "Interim"

Best be clear about it, early. What might be meant, in this context, by "City"? And, also, "interim"?

God chose to demonstrate through Calvin, Calvinists, and their impact upon the Western world that his Word can be preached into creation of that highest aspiration of wisdom, old and new and divine — the *City!* Creation of Word-inspired civil government. Better known just now, perhaps, as *community.* But Cicero preferred *civis* ... and Aristotle *polis* ... and St. Augustine *civitas Dei* ... and Calvin *Kingdom of Christ.* Always humankind at its best, the high road. The only kind God's Word knows!

And, for Calvinism, one example, from among almost countless attributions:

"It is safe to assume, then, that the influence of puritanism, in the broad Calvinistic sense, was a major force in the late colonial period, and that it contributed uniquely and profoundly to the making of the American mind when the American mind was in the making.... It was not surprising that patriotism was preached from the pulpits, and that political agitators would have drawn their inspiration from puritan ministers" (Perry, 359).

Pending further discussion, we can here profitably take note of how Calvin defines the doctrine of predestination:

"We call predestination God's eternal decree, by which he compacted with himself what he willed to become of each man. For all are not created in equal condition; rather eternal life is fore-ordained for some, eternal damnation for others. Therefore, as any man has been created to one or the other of these ends, we speak of him as predestined to life or to death" (*Institutes*, IV,21,5).

Bear in mind that for Calvin/Calvinists, the doctrine of predestination twice shapes the role assigned to Christianity in history. First, as Scripture reveals, God assigns the ultimate destiny of each of his Image-bearers, be it heaven or be it hell, from "before the foundation of the world" (Eph. 1:4). Calvin found that liberating. Ultimate human destinies rest not upon his shoulders, nor those of the Church, nor anyone's but God's. He finds freedom in that. He says, for example, "Whenever, then, the fewness of believers disturbs us, let the converse come to mind, that only those to whom it is given can comprehend the mysteries of God" (Calvin *Institutes*, I,7,5). Let's not be trying to mind God's business, however piously we phrase our excuse. Crusade evangelism is robbed of rationale. The pulpit has no heavenly mansions to give away. Nor can the Church assume authority to open heaven's gates.

Second, how is our real time to be spent, if celestial real estate is already in escrow?

It turned out to be Calvin's role in history to confront the world seriously with this question: IF ultimate destinies are indeed, yours and mine and everybody's, long settled, then what is left for the Church (and us) to be doing in the here and now and tomorrow? I call that the *interim*, what the poet calls "wisp of fog betwixt us and the sun," the number of sun-risings between birth and death. What's that for? In that small slice of time between the eternities allotted to each of us, what were we created to do, to seek, to want and desire? Most of us are in flight from facing that question, or finding answer, or judging what we are doing *right now* in its light. Maybe that's why there was a Calvin.

For Calvin, the answer is easy to grasp. The interim is the time to seek and do the Word-revealed will of the God who made, and judges, us. Not so easy to achieve. Turns out, as Calvin lived to show, that we need God, Word, and its proclamation to tackle it.

Cleansed by faith in Jesus Christ from the stain of Original Sin and liberated from the burdens of our own inherited and on-going trans-

gressions, we are freed to "know" (he pours much into the verb) God
and his ways to live the "interim" right. The "good news" of the Gospel
is that God provides for just that right Way. In Jesus Christ, we are *free*
to hear and *able* to seek the life to which all humankind is called, the life
of citizens in Christ's Kingdom, the *City,* liberated on Calvary, taught
and guided by the Word of God incarnate in the inspired Scripture and
preached by the Church. *That's the good news of the Gospel. That's what
Church and Word are for.* We could not repeat this too frequently, if we
are to understand Calvin's perception of his calling in God's Kingdom.
Calvin's Christianity is utilitarian. Life acquires meaning through taking the role assigned to each of us by talent and opportunity and destiny
to create, mostly by daily work — in the *interim* — what the ancient
Western mind called the "City."

Calvin writes in his letter to Cardinal Sadoleto that Christ "came to
render a people acceptable to God, zealous of good works. To the same
effect are many similar passages which prove that Christ came in order
that we, doing good works, might through him be accepted by God"
(*Reformation Debate,* 68).

Well, no, Calvin was not Luther! Both were well aware of it.

Calvin can say: "He particularly makes Himself Lord and King of
heaven and earth, because when He draws men to obedience by the
preaching of the Gospel, He is establishing the throne of His Kingdom upon earth" (*Commentary,* Matt. 28:20). Calvin preaches to es-
tablish the City, here and now, in time and place. Nothing else. Nothing less.

Notice how he unites the ancient Western vision with Christian reality. The City was sought by the "brightest and the best" across the
ages, especially in the West. The City comes close to hand where Christ
rules. And this rule is realized through the proclamation of his Word,
which is why his Body the Church is among us.

For Calvin, Gospel always implies Kingdom, here and now, with
echoes hereafter. Not, as for Catholicism and Luther, found by elevation
of the soul above, or escape from, the chaos of history. No, we are all
called to a Kingdom that is given existential possibility for everyone because Christ *does reign* in history through his Word *preached.* What

such preaching is, and does, is, as we shall see, the culminating theme of the *Institutes*.

Can everyone listen and *hear*?

It's been — of course — disputed, but for Calvin the burst of sunlit opportunity rising over Calvary omits no one. He makes a point of it in his *Catechism* of 1545: "But there is another kind of deliverance which applies equally to all men. For he has rescued us all from spiritual bondage to sin and from the dominion of the devil" (*Tracts and Treatises,* II, 57). No one omitted; no one forgotten! And what, then, of that "horrible decree" (the term is Calvin's) of reprobation? We'll visit its role as paradox in chapter 13-B.

In a comparison that Calvin likes to draw, humankind is liberated in Christ from bondage to Devil and death as all Israel was liberated by God from the Pharaoh and his Egypt. The risen Lord can send his Church out into the world to "go therefore and make disciples of all nations" by "teaching them to observe all that I have commanded you" (Matt. 28:19-20), knowing that depraved humankind *can* hear, thanks to Calvary, and *can* aspire to obey. His promise to be "with" such disciples underlies the achievements of the Word in the world to the end of time. Even if making "sense" of it all far outruns our best intellection.

The idea of the "City" is correlative to the idea of "Interim." It's our calling between eternities.

The idea of "City" is the human at communal best (unhappily also infested with the human at worst). It was hope of the greatest minds of the West long before perceptive description, say, in studies like Lewis Mumford's fine *The City in History*.

The *City:* what Pericles called his Athens, five centuries before Christ; what Plato called *The Republic,* and Aristotle described as the *Polis;* what Cicero fondly viewed as the *Civitas,* with its correlatives of *civil, civilized, civilization*. Visions long pursued. Visions coming nearest to realization in Western modernity through the Word preached from Calvin/Calvinist pulpits, preaching as prescribed in the culminating Book Four of the *Institutes*.

The *Calvinist City:* fruit of that creative Word that St. Paul was inspired to prefigure, say, in his *Romans* as its Constitution and in his

Galatians as declaration of independence; what St. Augustine's great treatise identified as *The City of God,* and Calvinists learned from Calvin's Geneva as seen through his *Institutes* to call Christ's *Kingdom,* finding installation by way of pulpits obedient to proclamation of the Word.

The *Calvinist City:* installed by Calvinists in Europe and then across the ocean, a believing citizenry thus discovering themselves to be the New Israel *elected* to create the long-anticipated "city set on a hill," (Matt. 5:14) — biblical description of the ancient secular expectation, civic entities substantiating the *Institutes,* and realizing in so doing something of Calvin's idea of Christian community.

The *Calvinist City:* witness to the all-pervasive grace of God. In perceiving, and preaching, how Christian pulpits can lend reality to that classic hope, John Calvin evokes the modern world. To believe that the Word *will,* preached into time and place, *real*ize humanity's highest communal aspirations, with fruits of obedience in time and eternity: *this is Calvinism!* Heaven can be tasted, here and now!

It is eminently arguable, indeed, that when Thomas Jefferson says that his phrasing for the *Declaration of Independence* was chosen from ideas "in the air" of his time, those ideas owed their ambiance to the Calvinist pulpits then thriving on the American scene.

The "Declaration" surely affirms what Puritans caught as the gleam in John Calvin's eye. Why else did he culminate his *Institutes* with tribute to civil government, and the sermon as vehicle for achieving its promise?

What else had he in view when he pens in his opening address to King Francis I: ". . . a very great question is at stake: how God's glory may be kept safe on earth, how God's truth may retain its place of honor, how Christ's Kingdom may be kept in good repair among us" (*Institutes,* 11). *Kept in good repair — from the pulpit — among us!* Calvinism!

The *Declaration* declares that democracy is the political face of a religious phenomenon. All people come in some sense equally into history, the *Declaration* says, by way of "creation." That concept can hardly be other than Christian, essentially Calvinist. Could, indeed, the very notion of a "Creator" who endows "all men" with *rights (!)* "inalienable" be common parlance except where Calvinist pulpits were speaking God's Word into the very air society breathed? And can the ideas of the *Declaration* really find footing in reality in any other context? How hollow and ineffectual "endowed by their Creator" echoes in a society grown secular, *where faith is willfully condemned to exile,* where Darwinism presumably substitutes for "creation," and "God" may be but a useful shorthand or handy expletive.

Jefferson's language is as much Calvinist/Genevan as it is too generally ignored. (The absurd shibboleth of "separation of church and state" derived mistakenly from Jefferson's "wall of separation" is as false to his intent, and to reality, as it is wholly unrealistic.)

The Word, which (or Who) called all things into being, entered the historical human family as Jesus the Christ also to weave the marvelous tapestry of Western democracy, widely done upon Calvinist looms.

Exempted by predestination from devoting energies to the "salvation of souls," Calvinism aims at the creation of Cities — with the destinies of souls long ago decided. Calvinist churches call those liberated on Calvary to take up the cross of self-denial for vocational obedience to the Law of God, preached as recipe for the City. Those elect to it can and will hear and heed. For such self-sacrifice the prime model is Calvin himself. The prime pattern is the world of the West.

Who Was He?

1. Geneva

We will come in a bit to such biography as we need, but for first encounter, this:

He's age 27. On the road to escape incineration by the Paris Inquisition whose indictment he had incurred. It is summer, August, 1536. He pauses for an overnight, troop movements — he says later, recounting the event — impeding his course to scholarly seclusion at Strasbourg.

The place is Geneva, somewhat en route from Paris to Strasbourg. It was a strange thing, really, quite the way providential events do take footing and seem to run off on their own. Here this greatly gifted man, already a formidable biblical scholar, dismounts at a then socially chaotic community of some thirteen thousand, Catholic Bishop recently expelled, now suffering severe disorder from the lifting of clerical regimen. As Hamlet says of *Hecuba,* what has he to do with Geneva, or Geneva with him?

That becomes the story of his life and of the rise of the Western world.

The visitor is violently confronted by the local Reformer, William Farel, and, most astonishingly, agrees to lay aside his cherished anticipation of quiet retreat into leisurely inconsequence. It was to be town, not gown, as his destiny. One thinks he knew it all along. Implies it in Book Four of the *Institutes* traveling with him. And despised the grime and grit of it. Most aristocratic of the Reformers, Barth says of him. Yes, it shows in that familiar Holbein portrait. Note the fur neckpiece. Just enough to show that he had a nice sensitivity to sartorial style.

He chooses to stay on. Already the vision of the City, writ deep in his soul as goal of history, begins to exercise its ancient fascination. *This is the place? And his Institutes the tool?* He knows that Christianity is given, not to escape life but to confront it. Already a brush with the Inquisition. If, as he knew, ultimate destiny is all settled by irrevocable predestination, then Christianity requires that mundane life is to be met head on, not fled. Life is to be focused, as Calvary was also endured, to draw close the *City,* sparkling among the accessible options of history. Why else God's gifts of life and time? That, he sees, is what the Church has been given the Word to promote. He looks through the visions of the wisest of the ancients to see their Cities evoked and matured by the love of God as defined in Augustine's *City of God* — already a favorite treatise — and determines to preach it into reality.

He knew it almost word for word, especially where Augustine writes,

"Accordingly, two cities have been formed by two loves: the earthly by the love of self; even to the contempt of God; the heavenly by the love of God; even to the contempt of self. The former, in a word, glories in itself, the latter in the Lord. For the one seeks glory from men; but the greatest glory of the other is God, the witness of conscience" (Augustine, 477). To settle such Cities in the *interim,* so the Church is called, today and always.

Augustine defines historical options. Calvin is, as well known, much influenced by him, illumined by Luchesius Smits in two substantial volumes, *Saint Augustine dans l'oeuvre de Calvin.* Who but God is capable of building the true City by *converting* love of self into love of God — and that by what revealed means other than his Word preached? Augustine knew; he taught Calvin, too. Cities can be perceived of such stuff as miracles dote on. And key to miracles is faith, created by God's biblical Word through the Holy Spirit. (You didn't know, or don't believe *that?* It's why Calvin lived. Come along a little and see more of him!)

Is that not why Christianity itself was given to the world, that the City should be raised upon the strands of time and place? And does not that "conversion" from *love of self* to *love of God* which is implied by Augustine explain all that Christianity is and does? Not conversion for sliding through pearly gates, but "salvation" out of self-absorption into self-denial and cross-bearing with City-making as consequence (Mark 8:34)? That, indeed, is what evangelism rallies should be all about — and aren't.

So, he stays — just say the towers of the world of the West are floating somewhere within the horizon of his anticipations. And he was finding historical footing in what was already Book Four of his great treatise.

He chose to stay. Why?

Well, say that he chose to draw up a chair, as Word-entrusted ambassador of the Most High, to the tumultuous table of Genevan (and then European) politics, to take a hand where stakes could run so high as to involve hatred, threats, exile, and even death. (All that, believing as he did in divine predestination. At that time he almost took it for granted as plain biblical revelation — only later it brewed up a storm.) He drew up to focus Christianity upon becoming what Spengler calls a "world power." Reminding us just a tiny bit of Quixote — always has. Forever driving by the Word into the very heart of things political, economic, social . . . ! And thus creating a City! That's what he stayed on to do . . . and did! And left behind "Calvinism" to carry on! It's all in the *Institutes!* Come see!

He came with that new *Institutes* in his saddle bag. God had chosen, there in 1536, unmistakably to initiate display of the democratic revolutionary potential of the Cross by putting that *Institutes* to immediate and hectic political trial. This done by settling the author into a rambunctious Geneva whilst the printer's ink was, so to speak, yet damp on its pages. Writer and treatise were put to test. And finally passed! The hard way!

In time, Geneva and his *Institutes* became reciprocal collaborators in democratizing towns, cities, even nations, to half the globe — the other half still to go. The "tool" Calvin learned exactly how to employ for that purpose was pulpit proclamation — *preaching* — of the divinely creative biblical Word which (or Who) hewed out of chaos, greed, and lethargy a half-world of political and social democracy, still preeminent candidate for driving history into glorious tomorrows.

In retrospect, Genevan University historian Charles Borgeaud can write in his history of Calvin's university, "Calvin had achieved his task: he had secured the future of Geneva . . . making it at once a church, a school, and a fortress. It was the first stronghold of liberty in modern times" (McNeill, 196).

So . . . he dismounted for an overnight. With a Spirit-dispatched messenger awaiting him to countermand that. He probably sensed it the moment he laid eyes on William Farel. For Calvin there was no coincidence; just Providence . . . and Mystery!

2. The Quarrel

There he is, mind you, quietly lodged, this August evening, in some Genevan hostelry. Suddenly he is accosted by the red-headed, rosy-bearded, intense Genevan Reformer, William Farel. We may surmise that the *Institutes* had won God's little race to get there before its writer.

Let's linger a moment on how Western democratic transcendence found entrance upon mundane time and space.

Someone whispers, "That man John Calvin is *here!*" Farel, fresh from glancing into the *Institutes,* trembling in anticipation, almost unbelieving, hastens (of course) to that man's overnight location.

Yes, there he found him!

Can this be he? The man who wrote this book? Here, in flesh and blood? No less?

Get him!!

Yes, the Spirit led them to historic encounter there — both believed that. Of course, Farel shouted. Of course, he strode back and forth, his voice echoing out to the hallways of the place, something like this perhaps:

You, Sir, must be the very man whom God has sent at this hour of Geneva's peril and urgent need!

The visitor does not seem to hear.

[Into his face, then]: *Did you not write this?* **Do all things in the Word?** [Oh, so he had looked into the book!] *What have you been waiting for? What are you going to do about it, now that God has brought you here?*

Were you hiding from yourself, there in Strasbourg? How dare you? Do you fancy God asleep? Have you no sense of awe? Of liberating fear? We have a St. Peter's pulpit here [You do get the point? Rome has one, too.] *for one who could compose this treatise. Take it! Or be forever cursed by the God betrayed by your cowardice!* [Aimed to strike home! With a whisper from the Spirit, Farel read him at once.] *Show us how clearly you see, in the Light of that Word, Sir, our situation! You are at the heart of reformation of the Church here.* [You get it? All excitement, all open to change!] *We are at it, here and now! Yes, do all things . . . how right, how very right. . . . Revealed to you before you came! All in the Word! Exactly the prescription for our troubles. And promise to all our hopes. Praise God . . . stay here and apply it!*

The visitor wriggles. But cannot leave. Everything he had read and written conspired to teach him one thing: Christianity can — Christ having lived, died, and risen again — facilitate the next step toward the realization, beginning there and then in Switzerland, of the ancient vision of *City,* humanity's highest mundane anticipation. Long seen as the human community where, in neat reciprocation, each gave according to ability and received according to need. Oh, how many centuries of fervent hope! (Marx later claimed that for his "classless society," but Marxists corrupted it into tyranny; Calvin did much better in his Geneva, and countless Calvinists in other climes after him.)

John Calvin stayed on, with far greater consequence for your world and mine than we are apt to know, so many historians as blind-sided to Providence as they are apt to be.

Always chary of personal references, Calvin did leave a laconic account of this epic event in the Preface to his commentary on the Psalms. He probably put it there because the Psalms was a favorite biblical book for him; David's God-amended misadventures, so often, he thought, illumined his to himself. In consequence, Calvin is more autobiographical there than usually so:

> William Farel detained me at Geneva, not so much by counsel and exhortation, as by a dreadful imprecation, which I felt to be as if God had from heaven laid his mighty hand upon me to ar-

rest me. As the most direct road to Strasbourg, to which I intended to retire, was shut up by the wars, I had resolved to pass quickly by Geneva, without staying longer than a single night in that city. A little before this, Popery had been driven from it by the exertions of the excellent person whom I have named, and Peter Viret; but matters were not yet brought to a settled state, and the city was divided into unholy and dangerous factions. Then an individual who now basely apostatized and returned to the Papists, discovered me and made me known to others. Upon this, Farel, who burned with extraordinary zeal to advance the gospel, immediately strained every nerve to detain me.

And after having learned that my heart was set upon devoting myself to private studies, for which I wished to keep myself free from other pursuits, and finding that he gained nothing by entreaties, he proceeded to utter an imprecation that God would curse my retirement, and the tranquility of the studies which I sought, if I should withdraw and refuse assistance, when the necessity was so urgent. By this imprecation I was so stricken with terror, that I desisted from the journey which I had undertaken; but sensible of my natural bashfulness and timidity, I would not bring myself under obligation to discharge any particular office (Preface, *Commentary, Psalms,* I, xlii).

No words wasted. This is the man God greatly gifted and then bent to his bidding. Biographer Jean Cadier entitles his account, *The Man God Mastered.* This was the crossroad where Christianity took on world politics — democratically, *from the people up,* via the pulpit. And, Calvinism the best, if not the only, form for the hope that humankind still has for creative common exploitation of the vast natural resources that God sets to human hand in his pulsating universe.

Two men. Two transcending types. Two God-elected sluice gates to flow Light and Power into time, place, and circumstance. A William Farel, a John Calvin, and predetermined destiny.

Let's pause here, and muse just a little. Try sharing Calvin's vision of how far-reaching could be the civilization available tomorrow on humankind's exploiting by Genesis command ("subdue the earth" [Gen. 1:28]) the natural prodigality God scatters in his world. Envision the broader, deeper, higher culture and civilization, souls maturing along the way, if Christian energies, neglected altogether or misused now in campaign evangelism, were instead spent upon sober, courageous, indefatigable proclamation of the heavenly Word, vibrant in the inspired Book, just after the manner of Calvin and Calvinists.

Envision with the "brightest and the best" the exploitation of what Pericles saw in his Athens, five centuries before Christ; what the Greek sages meant by "know thyself" two centuries earlier; and what others of the gifted visionaries we have already noted saw. All made correlative to the liberating revelation of divine predestination, not as substance of theological hair-splitting, but as motivation to *interim* creation of the Kingdom of Christ, here and now, *heaven already taken*. History is all we have to call our own. Calvin saw that, read the Bible accordingly, and preached the Word as masterful Guide.

From Calvary to City! Because all are freed in the Cross, therefore all who will can add their bit to the City, energized out of the Word-preached. Calvinism!

How casually he recalls it, the fulcrum that changed everything — for him and for his world and ours. He never lost the tantalizing vision of the true City, catching the eye of genius, well over two centuries before the Declaration of Independence. Surely, as already said, that momentous document was the creation of the Word so widely preached from Calvinist pulpits in Jefferson's time and place. (He was a Deist, you say? Ah, but he credits the sentiments of his great enunciation to ideas "in the air" — preached there, surely, from Calvinist pulpits! "Created equal" is hardly Deism is it?)

Peek at our world now, via TV and news media and internet. How rich, how varied, how unbelievably abundant — and yet, how chaotic, how violent, how demon-beset, how many deprived, how vast the talents wasted. How riven by tension, rebellion, hatred. Is there no panacea? No comprehensive alternative? No Word . . . ?

Oh, yes. A WORD! Just what we need; and all we need! Glance at that Book there, your Bible. Incarnate in it is a Word seeking its (his) own incarnation in our selves and behavior, via the pulpit. For *everyone.* Far excelling the elitist expectations of Western genius, let alone the grubby hand of ideologues.

Oh yes, there is urgency, was then and is now. Let's ask ourselves what Power we think might create *civis* out of all we see and hear about us. What strength might lay order upon what swirls as in the wind, locally and abroad? What decisive, courageous alternative to those who, like a Lenin, turn to force for solutions? Or secret police, Gulag, torture, executions, spies on every street, lies debilitating language? Yes indeed, those are the techniques-in-trade of the ideologue, be it Marxist, Fascist, Nazi, or other apostles of the totalitarian. "Force," says one of Lenin's most recent biographers in a highly perceptive study, "was always for him the favorite social and political weapon" (Volkogonov, 69), one ruthlessly applied. The demonic writhes everywhere. Hatred and violence in grim and deadly operation. Evil ever leering.

But brutal, physical force was not to be Calvin's tactic, though he advocated just war where required. For him life is battle, spiritual conflict overlying the physical. Power of God versus power of Devil. Struggle was spiritual, highest level, with blood and sword not excepted, though ever under spirit. The West is not the outgrowth of ideological fancy or tyrant's tactics. Could the muddied Marxist fountain bubble up freedom? It hasn't so far, let professors toy with it as they will.

So then, what "assistance" to Farel is he competent to offer?

That's in his *Institutes.*

For now, consider: What if you were led to believe, as profoundly as you believe yourself to exist, that God has spoken, and put on record all that a flourishing democracy needs? That within the covers of the Bible there on your table, incarnate in the syllables of our own language, throbs the *living Word of God?* Calvin calls *Word* "the everlasting Wisdom, residing with God from which all oracles and prophecies go forth" (*Institutes,* I,13,6). And he had written an *Institutes of the Christian Religion* to affirm that, to trace out its course and consequences, showing what the *Word* has done, and can do for humankind in the here, now, and always.

There can be no understanding, nor appreciation, of him and his immense influence unless we adapt to seeing the Bible as he saw it. Yes, that Book. Nothing special? Just another amidst the avalanche pouring off the presses? But that's not all that John Calvin saw, in letting the Book lead him into becoming a "world power." Ignore for a while, if you can, the baggage imposed upon your Bible by the "learned," the elitist, the "cutting-edge" types. Here, in your hand, is the linguistic incarnation of the Word which (or better Who — it's both) once called creation into being, the Word Who underlies and animates that creation, Who died and rose to liberate a human race bound by sin, Who vibrantly sustains and expands all creation still, and has the capacity (that's what Calvin and Calvinism proclaim) to create vigorous temporal civilization not yet envisioned. The West was Word-created, not stumbled upon. Look about you, and behold its dimensions. Take courage. What God has once done, he can and will repeat. So Calvin taught and lived.

See our freedom and civilization as fruit of the Word John Calvin found incarnate in the Bible, waiting to take further incarnation in selves and institutions around the globe. Such is the exciting anticipation implicit in the heritage of the man who served Western history as agent for, and (just perhaps) the pre–Don Quixote of that Book!

Think a moment on the many-paged struggle that Karl Barth, genius as he was, wages early in his *Church Dogmatics* to assure himself that the Bible, in some sense, speaks true. And then compare that with Calvin's crisp affirmation: "Scripture exhibits fully as clear evidence of its own truth as white and black things do of their color, or sweet and bitter of their taste" (*Institutes*, I,7,3). Take it or leave it! That's how he preached. Soul of the West!

And what, too, if we also join him in believing that this very Word — by no license from science, from research, from clever people — is made *commonly* available — to the wisest and the simplest (there may be no real distinction between these here) through *faith* for providing the Light to see life by, and the Power to live it right. And that *practical* schooling in this Word is what, and is all, that the Church is given to do — faith being created by "hearing . . . the word . . ." (Rom. 10:17, KJV). To find, with him, that "All right knowledge of God is born of obedience" (*Institutes*, I,6,2), the obedience which flowers in Cities.

But . . . there is "science." Does it give us license these days to accept as true and accurate that ancient Book?

Ah, that temptation is of old time! Calvin knew it well, of course. It worked in the beginning. "Did God say . . . ?" (Gen. 3:1) was, and ever remains, the first challenge. Calvin disposed of it briskly: "All the sciences which men may teach us are no better than smoke; it is a transitory thing which is soon vanished" (*Sermons*, Ps. 119).

Might not there be, given vision enough, and will for it, such a thing for Calvinists of tomorrow as a National Pulpit, even one "Internetional"? Not to fleece the gullible; not to advertise the preacher; but just for *preaching*, like a Calvin, the Word of God into the very stuff of history? No fuss. No pleas. Just preaching. An intention evoked by the transcendent vision inherent in vintage Calvin and Calvinism to substantiate expansion of the world of the West. Not a crusade to "save" souls! That's not, never was, John Calvin. But, why do we suppose a fore-thoughtful Providence has now provided humankind with internets and such, like tentacles embracing continents? Only as toys? For trade? Always for the grubby? Is vision totally fled from the Church?

Is there not far more, far greater, potential resident in the creation than has yet been developed, patiently waiting upon Word-driven, not "science"-shackled, apostles?

3. Before . . . *and* . . . After

Say we owe it to ourselves and to him to ask with what success Calvin survived Geneva, and it him.

Yes, he had signed on. The military patois often characterized his language and his mood. Life was, for him, constant battle with the demonic. The Adversary active in the Fall was busy everywhere, every-how, every-when. Seeing the claw of the Devil where it is well-hidden helped him focus energy and enlist draftees. Too bad the bland, the indiscriminate protects the Devil so often and so arrogantly.

Calvin believed that the Word-*preached* effected the momentous change that Geneva experienced between its condition at his arrival and its status when his life drew to its close.

What indeed was the town like when he came, and the City like when he left? What had the Word-*preached* made of his Geneva?

The sword of his tongue at first turned so much of the Genevan world upside down as to agitate agents of the Enemy eager to expel, or as he feared sometimes, to destroy him. And in less than two years of his kind of pulpitry, he was on the road again. Expelled! Relieved and even happy . . . at first.

Looking back out of exile, he writes to Pastor James Bernard, still preaching in Geneva: "Above all, do you seriously consider that you are engaged in the discharge of an office, which, as it excels every other, so it is the most dangerous of all, if you do apply yourself with the utmost diligence and intensity to the duties belonging to it. If you care for my approval, I would forewarn you of this one thing, that I require no more of you than that you devote yourself sincerely and faithfully to the Lord" (*Letters,* I, 237).

Has the world, or the Word, or the Devil so much changed that no one is likely to associate the pulpit, now, with danger at all — save in totalitarian states? Which is damningly instructive, really. But there is that qualification that can make the pulpit threatening, *"If you do apply yourself with the utmost diligence and intensity to the duties belonging to it."* Well, yes, IF . . .

With him into exile went colleagues Farel and blind Courault, in the spring of 1538. Sent off with threats and curses. On to Strasbourg after all, where a French-speaking congregation was provided for him. But Geneva was ever on his mind. His correspondence during the exile years is a study in contrasts and tensions — revulsion at the maltreatment he endured, fear of the physical threats, contempt of the trickery, playing off against *duty* to the Church, which had made him one of her pastors, and determination to see that Church thrive in course.

In due season he was drawn back, both against and yet by his wishes, in 1541. And then he fought out adverse reactions to his exertions to create a City, until a failed Enemy attempt at revolution and a turn in local politics gave him finally, in 1555, supportive backing in the Council. It was safer thereafter, less physically threatening, but no less strenuous. The Word was given more elbow-room to work. Nine years left.

What was Geneva like when Calvin first arrived there, that scented summer afternoon in 1536, his heart (not on track with God's, as he found out) so eager for leisure, his mind set for scholarship?

Did he soon realize that Geneva was to be in fact the kind of place God chose as challenge to his *Institutes?* To show just what might be made of chaotic Geneva, by way of Calvin's absolute trust in the Word he had already so thoroughly studied and so comprehensively focused upon the Kingdom?

Did he foresee a "harvest of souls" there? Did he fashion evangelistic crusades? Not he; not Calvinism. Hardly within the scope of predestination, twist that as expositors do.

Crusadism was never his way. The Bible was his master, not his servant. Geneva promoted no mission enterprises, not as local crusades nor as foreign ventures. (One incidental attempt, in Brazil, amounted to nothing.) What evidence is there — has there ever been — that gospel crusades, or mega-churches, or TV huckstering contribute to *City*-creation? There were, indeed, pastors sent into France to destabilize the harsh government of Francis I. And when, after his death, a new King filed complaint with the Council of Geneva, Calvin seems to have misled them on the facts. (Robert M. Kingdon has a fine account of it all in his *Geneva and the Coming of the Wars of Religion in France.*)

He arrived, was expelled, and returned, not for mission but for revolution! Not for heaven but for interim, history, and City. His *Institutes* was prescript for City-making. His focus already spells out very precisely what civil government is *for* — to sinew the City. And he finds that Geneva poses him the question, "Did you get it right? Is that what preaching Christianity really can do? Really is *for?*"

The answer to that question is the story of Geneva, and of the West.

And, yes, he had it right. He lived long enough to know. He learned that God's Word preached according to the *Institutes* is exactly the key that opens history *democratically* to ancient aspirations, on Calvary made historically available to everyone! The Word transcends the class lines that held the ancients in bond.

His seemingly fortuitous overnight was not by happenstance, of course. Providence knows nothing of the accidental. Things just look that way sometimes. Geneva confronted him precisely to reveal just how *politically useful* was — and *is* — the Christianity of that *Institutes* in all the hurly-burly of everyday life. What kind of City could God's Word courageously proclaimed make? (In exactly the same way the trauma of Communist states openly advertises the deadly misconceptions of reality in *Das Kapital!*)

The Geneva to which he came was described by his distinguished colleague Theodor Beza, as disorderly, chaotic, ridden by faction:

> Though the Gospel had been received into the city, and popery
> abjured, many disgraceful crimes still continued to reign among

various persons in a city which had been for many years under the power of monks, and of a profligate clergy; and ancient quarrels were still fostered among some of the principal families. . . . The evil increased so much that the city was divided by the seditious conduct of private individuals into various factions. . . (18-19).

Modern historian E. William Monter describes that Geneva, after the expulsion of its reigning Bishop in 1535: "Her first five years of independence, which culminates in a showdown between rival political factions in 1540, was unmitigated chaos, a tragicomedy acted out by exuberant amateurs" (64).

—————— ∞ ——————

That's what faced him, after he yielded to Farel's entreaties.

With only Bible and *Institutes* in hand (quite an armory, really), John Calvin strides into a veritable social wilderness, in spirit and content not unlike what his Puritan spiritual descendants faced upon the rocky coast of New England in the next century — wild, rugged, treacherous, dangerous.

—————— ∞ ——————

And what, then, after struggle, temporary defeat, and renewed effort, did Calvin leave behind as he departed both Geneva and life together in May, 1564? Did he (or did the Word) succeed in *realizing* the dream? How effective was his blueprint?

German sociologist/theologian Ernst Troeltsch reports:

Here then — for the first time in the history of the Christian ethic — there came into existence a Christian Church whose social influence, as far as it was possible at that period, was completely comprehensive. As we have already seen, Calvinism was "Christian Socialism," in the sense that it molded in a corporate way the whole life in the State and in Society, in the Family, and in the economic sphere, in public and in private, in accordance with Christian standards. It took care that every individual member should receive his appointed share of the natural and spiritual possessions of the community, while at the same time it sought to make the whole of Society, down to the smallest level, a real expression of the royal dominion of Christ. . . . As already indicated, this "Christian Socialism" was quite different from its modern counterpart of any kind. . . . Indeed, the great importance of the Calvinistic social theory does not consist merely in the fact that it is one great type of Christian social doctrine; its significance is due to the fact that it is one of the great types of sociological thought in general. In inner significance and historical power the types of French optimistic equalitarian democracy, of State Socialism, of totalitarian Communist Socialism, and of the mere theory of power, are, in comparison with Calvinism, far behind (II, 622).

That last sentence is instructive. Among revolutionary options Christianity, à la Calvin, is *primus inter pares!*

Summarized by Professor W. M. Southgate in his biography of English Bishop John Jewel, "Equal in significance and importance to his [Calvin's] writings, is his other masterpiece, the city of Geneva. As a capital of Reformed Protestantism and a model for Christian society, it, like the *Institutes,* had no rival" (165).

And Geneva was illustrated in time by the world of the West.

The *Institutes* met and brilliantly passed the ultimate test: It worked!

The City can be preached into existence. It was preached into existence. That is, as Calvin saw it, what Word, Church, and preaching are given for.

That is the indubitable witness through history of Calvin and his City, and the vast achievement of the West. It could be augmented now, and spread around the globe. It must be. Now, lest the night descend!

That's why the *Institutes* was conceived and put into language so vivid and authoritative as to take position among the great books of all time. Calvin aptly profiles how the ruling Lord exercises his authority: the pulpit as Throne of the Christ in the midst of his City!

William Haller pictures what the Calvinist Puritans over two centuries later envisioned when they thought of Calvin's City: "The reformers or Puritans were Calvinists . . . supported by the success of the state which Calvin's genius had called into being in Geneva. . . . They had seen what appeared to be Utopia founded on the word of God. . . . The key to Calvinistic reasoning was that the Bible gave a rule to be followed in church and state as in all other affairs in life. The real energy of the movement was supplied by the preacher, whatever his party or sect" (8, 14-15).

And surely he came to see, as his Geneva first expelled and then embraced him, that the ancient dream of the "City" was itself prophetic, blind as philosophers may commonly be to that. It is most nearly achieved by the Spirit's creative incarnation of God's Word preached into human behavior. And, even now, syllables of God's Word, ever re-echoing in Calvinist-oriented society in countless forms and formulations, creating its own ambiance, fashion the spiritual environment that characterizes the West — far from perfection, but withal quite obviously the nearest humankind has yet attained to the noblest of human communal aspirations.

There is more to be seen in Calvin and Calvinism, Horatio . . .

4. As Cromwell Saw

A chaotic populace finds order and focus en route to becoming a City.

God puts his Word at Calvin's disposal (which is exactly how Calvin viewed it, as he will reveal how in Book Four) to fashion out of chaotic Geneva a **City**, noblest of human social accomplishments.

Ah, the *City!* Must not that idea be the source of the irresistible revolutionary attraction exuded by the sobriquet "citizen" for the revolutionaries of many times? Syllables of hope and aspiration!

Unless some vision of the City be in the background, how else could the term "citizen" exercise its magical impulsion? And what Power, as Calvin believed and demonstrated, more concretely universalized and democratized the City than that of the creative Word of the living God, sent on its (his) Way from Christian pulpits?

No one can have stressed more succinctly, as Calvin himself employed it, the *vehicle* he was given for City-creation than did Calvinist soldier-statesman Oliver Cromwell (1599-1658), a century after Calvin. He, in his brief tenure as Lord Protector of England (1653-58), spread much of the complexion of on-coming democracy upon the England of his era. He led his cavalry into battle with Genevan psalms upon his lips, hearty laughter following after. This man was brought to wide attention by Thomas Carlyle in the nineteenth century, and comes vividly alive in Lady Antonia Fraser's sprightly biography *The Lord Protector*. He is also reckoned *God's Englishman* by left-leaning historian Christopher Hill, in a generally appreciative study.

Cromwell saw the Christian life, after Calvin, as a City-fying *this-worldly* fruit of God's Word preached. He saw a Christianity active in the streets, normative in the halls of decision, citizens compelled, propelled, impelled by Spirit and inspired language. Both men perceived Christianity as given to set the relationships of daily life in the Light of revelation, touching the common with uncommon significance, surfacing in the great Cities of the West. They were as acutely sensitive to divinely motivated social dynamics as the contemporary secular political "expert" is uniquely self-blinded to them.

Returned from subduing unrest in Scotland in 1650, Cromwell writes, in language that might have been Calvin's, from his Whitehall palace on September 9 to Governor Dundas in the Castle of Edinburgh, of some ministers who had hidden there from battle:

When they purely trust to the Sword of the Spirit which is the Word of God, which is powerful to bring down strongholds and every imagination that exalts itself — which alone is able to square and fit the stones for the new Jerusalem — then and not before, and by that means and no other, shall Jerusalem, the City of the Lord, which is to be the praise of the whole earth, be built; the Sion of the Holy One of Israel. (Carlyle, VIII, 60)

A veritable text to Calvinism! The vision of the *Institutes* could not be more succinctly put, nor prescription for Calvinist preaching more vividly enunciated.

"When they purely trust to the Sword of the Spirit . . ." yes, and when the Church displays such trust in pulpits preaching the Bible as "the very lips of God" — this phrase is Calvin's.

Thus says Calvin: "So when Jesus Christ causes His Gospel to be preached in a country, it is as if He said, '*I want to rule over you and be your King*'" (*Sermons,* Acts 1:1-4).

The English warrior-statesman catches precisely the mind and spirit that animated Calvin's foray into the thickets of Genevan (and broader) politics, and Calvin's courageous determination to preach into a faction-ridden chaos the lineaments of the **City**, coming finally to extend in effect around half the world. His Geneva becomes the model-precursor of the Cities made by the Word through Calvinists into basic constituents of Western culture.

But let us take admonition from how confused in vision the cities of the West appear now from absence of adequate, on-going, biblical pulpit nourishment. Doesn't the citizenry — while its presumed "leadership" looks busily some other way — seem to wait well-nigh breathlessly upon the appearance of another "Calvin" borne upon a tide of divine circumstance?

Retrospect

5. Noyon to Failure — 1509-1538

The spare, intense man, making his way from Berne to Strasbourg in the spring of 1538, perhaps on a mule, or perhaps in a conveyance shared with his brother and sister, was, we might suppose, communing thus with himself:

"If God designs to use his Word to create, sustain, and govern his universe, teeming with life, exploding with energy, infinite in beauty, why should he not with the same Word subdue the reckless willfulness of his fallen and wayward Image-bearers and thus lay civic order upon the affairs of those to whom he has given the planet? If, indeed, he offers us access to the Light and Power of that Word in his own way? But what is that way? And where did we miss it?"

We may imagine John Calvin thus moodily reflecting as he moved slowly toward Strasbourg, having been summarily expelled from Geneva on April 23, in the year of our Lord 1538, and curtly refused right to return when he appealed from Berne a few days later. He was *out!* The Devil's brew on which Geneva had malnourished the last two years of his life was now escaped. Free! Free at last! Liberated from confrontation with those to whom "it was a matter of entire indifference," he writes in his Preface to his commentary on the Psalms, "although the Church should sink into ruin, provided they obtained what they sought — the power of acting just as they pleased" — a species never uncommon.

He goes on to say in this Preface that he had "rejoiced more than it

25

became me, when, in consequence of certain commotions, I was banished from Geneva." Commotions, indeed, not excluding threats upon his life. Rejoiced, ah yes, but not so free a hand as he had anticipated. Failure leaves its scars. Farel and he had been just learning to grasp the dimensions of refashioning a miscellany of people into a City when the political maneuvering, of which he was yet to become a master, had outdone them. He could not forget. How humiliating! Had God deserted him? Or had he failed God? The query half-answered itself.

He came, in time, to count that defeat as "part of my early training," not for the life of scholarship but in City-building, on the premises, by the Word. It was ever so for him. God prodding him to extend his reach beyond his grasp, with inevitable demonic (he never doubted that) reaction.

⸙

As he mused, his life passed quickly by.

He reflected that the studious course he had set himself from adolescence onward had been interrupted from time to time by unwelcome obligation. He had at crucial junctures felt obliged to do what he did not want to do, always with the sense that God's will was involved and guiding him, sometimes contrary to his own. (French writer Jean Cadier entitles his biography *The Man God Mastered,* the French perhaps allowing "pummeled").

He muses on his birth (July 10, 1509) into the family of Gérard Cauvin, probably a notary, of Noyon. Boyhood and youth had passed smoothly enough, save for the traumatic loss of his mother when he was only four. Jeanne de la Franc was esteemed for her beauty and her piety when Gérard Cauvin had married her. Jean, as he was baptized, had but briefly known his mother, who was characterized — 'twas said — by a deep sense of piety and duty to God and neighbor, and by a desire to serve Church and society in God's name, traits early known of Jean.

His private education with the sons of a wealthy family, the Mommors, had early revealed his precocious gifts, and the local Bishop de Hangst had singled him out for training in Paris on a stipend leading to the priesthood. At age fourteen he, with his classmates, went to Paris to pursue the liberal studies that already much attracted him, the great Erasmus (1466?-1536) a likely model to be emulated or even excelled.

Already a career of scholarly disinvolvement seemed within his grasp, and his work in the several schools he attended was done so well as sometimes to include, according to his colleague Beza, teaching classes he was enrolled to take. At nineteen he had a Master's degree. Already the career of the scholar glimmered within reach. And then his father had a falling out with the Bishop of Noyon.

Not the priesthood but the law, his father decreed, would be Jean's future. More money in it. Frustrated but obedient, he had gone first to Orléans to study case law with one Pierre d'Estoile, best of his time in that; and then to Bourges to study legal theory with one Alciati, no less distinguished. A doctorate, free of charge, Beza says, came out of those two years. The training was useful to City-making. It helped when the Council of Geneva assigned him the task of codifying the city's laws. It fine-tuned a mind gifted for argument and disputation. And it no less stimulated his determination to try his hand at scholarly recognition.

Ford Battles examines in some detail the rungs on the scholarly ladder as Calvin mounted them, in the first chapter of his (posthumous) *Interpreting John Calvin*. Oh yes, he was up to it — Erasmus, move over! Calvin remembered vividly every page he ever read, Beza says. And once, in the boot camp he thought his first Geneva experience, he totally humiliated a reckless ex-monk named Bolsec by quoting perfectly from memory, to his purposes, Church Fathers his critic had tried to use against him. Bolsec never forgot, nor forgave, and fathered a school of Calvin-vituperation, which has to this day its own history.

The going path to distinction for learning, invitingly open, was at that time carved out by composition of some learned commentary upon a classic treatise. Eagerly he takes the path, influenced perhaps by his growing predilection for the idea of "City."

His choice of scholarly vehicle is to do a commentary on the "De Clementia" of the Roman Stoic philosopher Seneca (4 B.C.–65 A.D.), written to soften the Emperor Nero's brutal lineaments of character. While doing the treatise in Latin, he comes to Latinize his name as Johannes Calvinus.

The youthful scholar's commentary was done à la mode: "He shows himself," writes Allan Menzies, "acquainted with the whole of Greek and Latin classical literature, citing 155 Latin authors and twenty-two Greek, and citing them with understanding" (137-38). The classic exponents of the "City" roamed freely about in his mind.

Heinrich Berger argues persuasively in *Calvin's Geschichts-auffassung* that the young Calvin had in mind more than scholarly repute in his exhaustive wrestling with political theory in the light of Seneca's treatise. He is also, Berger thinks, speaking to his times in critiquing the parallels to Nero in the abuse of political power by prevailing tyrannies, beginning with the rule of Francis I in Calvin's own France. It was, in any case, Calvin's first gesture in the direction of seizing scholarly notoriety, one he took so seriously as to publish his thesis at his own expense.

His exhaustive research in classic political philosophy no doubt served the inclination that came to focus in his *Institutes,* namely that Christianity makes civil government noblest of the "callings" open to man.

Calvin's father dies in May, 1531. Now John hastens with his Seneca manuscript back to Paris. By February of 1532 he has the *Commentary* complete, and in print . . . and paid for.

Under date of May 23, 1532, he writes from Paris to Francis Daniel, former fellow student at Orléans:

> Well, at length the die is cast. My Commentaries on the Books of Seneca, *De Clementia,* have been printed, but at my own expense, and have drawn from me more money than you can well suppose. At present, I am using every endeavor to collect some of it back. I have stirred up some of the professors of this city to make use of them in lecturing. In the University of Bourges I have induced a

friend to do this from the pulpit by a public lecture. You can also help me not a little. If you will not take it amiss; you will do so on the score of our old friendship; especially as, without any damage to your reputation, you may do me this service, which will also tend perhaps to the public good. Should you determine to oblige me by this benefit, I will send you a hundred copies, or as many as you please. Meanwhile, accept this copy for yourself, while you are not to suppose that by your acceptance of it, I hold you engaged to do what I ask. It is my wish that all may be free and unconstrained between us (*Letters*, I, 31-32).

The fickle scholarly mill casts the dedicated aspirant rudely aside. It seems that little recognition was elicited from the critics, scholarly or otherwise. It may be problematic whether Calvin ever did recoup his investment in learned repute. A fine modern edition, copiously supplemented with Introduction and notes, done by Ford Battles and André Malan Hugo is to hand in 448 pages. Of these, Calvin's Latin text, with English translation on facing page, extends from pages 140 to 380. (The editors believe that the letter to Francis Daniel quoted above was in fact written to one Philippe du Laurier, bookseller at Orléans, April 22, 1532. They authenticate, however, two further letters involving Daniel, one to him saying essentially the same thing as quoted above, and one from him to Calvin offering to assist in every way he can [387-391].)

———— ∞ ————

The Seneca commentary produced but a tiny splash. The door to acclaim hinging upon scholarly recognition remained stubbornly closed against him. But another opened.

His close friend, Nicolas Cop, son of William Cop, the royal physician to French King Francis I (which suggests that Calvin had frequented the royal palace of the King whom he later addressed by introductory letter to his *Institutes*), was on the staff of that theological arm of the University of Paris called the Sorbonne and was to be Rector for the year 1533-34. Calvin had gone with him to play some role there, and when Cop was obliged to prepare the annual Rectorial address for All Saints' Day, 1533, they composed it together — or, as some say, Calvin did it alone. Is Erasmus one step closer?

Not for long.

Luther's by-then notorious 1517 posting of ninety-five theses on the door of his Wittenberg chapel was already old news, but it had touched off what became widespread Catholic "heresy" hunting, with imprisonment, torture, and death devised to stamp it out. Not least involved in the process was the Inquisition of Paris, supported by powerful members of the Parliament and lately by King Francis I. And, in the "affair of the placards," pro-Lutheran theses had been affixed to Parisian walls, not excluding the bedroom door of the King.

The sensitive nose of the Inquisitor sniffed "Lutheranism" in Cop's address, and the acrid odor led not only to the Rector but to Calvin. Warned just in time, the two fled their respective dwellings in haste, Calvin by way of a back window as the gendarmes came in the front door, all possessions, books and manuscripts included, remaining behind.

He had rushed in where an Erasmus had prudently declined to tread. He had knowingly identified himself as candidate for purification by fire. The potential Erasmus acquired a repute he neither sought nor avoided, and found himself a hunted fugitive. Calvin was obliged to spend the next several years moving from place to place, including a jaunt to Italy for visiting the Queen of Ferrara. Postponed was that secluded and quiet scholarly retreat. In process was that "training" he may have sensed was being imposed upon him.

The part of Cop's address that set inquisitorial noses twitching went like this:

"Blessed will you be," he [Jesus] says, "when men hurl insults at you and reproach you, and say all evil against you falsely, for my sake." Why, then, do we conceal the truth rather than speak it out boldly? Is it right to please men rather than God; to fear those who can destroy the body, but not the soul? O the ingratitude of mankind which will not bear the slightest affliction in the name of him who died for the sins of all, him whose blood has freed us from eternal death and the shackles of Satan! The world and the wicked are wont to label as heretics, impostors, seducers and evil-speakers those who strive purely and sincerely to penetrate the minds of believers with the Gospel; "they think they are offering service to God." But happy and blessed are they who endure all this with composure, giving thanks to God in the midst of affliction and bravely bearing calamities. "Rejoice," he says, "for great is your reward in heaven" (quoted in Introduction to F. L. Battles translation of the 1536 edition of Calvin's *Institutes,* v).

The speech illumines the cast of mind developing within him that led Calvin out of the quiet shadows of scholarship and into the life of civic encounter that commitment to God, as he came to see it, made, for him, obligatory. The Christian is not without obligation to the cause of the oppressed, however exercised. And the reaction to it prefigured experiences awaiting him in Geneva. The Erasmian life steadily waned in fascination. Experience was the divinely crafted tool for seeing to that. It was, for him, often so, theory and ideas hounded by God-imposed politico-social realities.

Had the candidate for the priesthood become "Lutheran" in his understanding of Christianity? Yes, but in his own way, one which led him further and further from Lutheranism as experience unfolded the civic indifference hidden in "by faith alone," until near the end of his life he refers to Lutheranism as "that evil," and vows to oppose its spread in every possible way (*Letters,* IV, 322).

When, and how, was John Calvin "converted" from Catholicism for the first time? There is, one almost says of course, sharp difference of opinion about it — detailed, for example, in studies like Catholic Alexandre Ganoczy's *Le jeune Calvin* and Fritz Buser's *Die Rätsel um die Bekehrung Calvins,* and commented upon by many biographers. Calvin himself affords two accounts of how it occurred: (1) in his exchange of letters, while residing in Strasbourg, with Catholic Cardinal Sadoleto, where Calvin justifies the role of one (presumably meaning himself) coming fresh to Reform; and (2) in the (rare) autobiographical comments given in his Introduction to *Commentary on the Psalms.*

What is puzzling about these two versions is that in the first he seems to suggest a somewhat slow process of his own departure from Catholicism, while in the second it is referenced as sudden and overwhelming. But, since transformation there was, why need we join the speculation over how it took place? Small matter, really. He could have done well enough for himself had he remained in Sadoleto's communion, he tells the Cardinal.

He did, in 1534, resign his Noyon benefice. Later in Basle he completed the first edition of his *Institutes,* destined to become one of the so-called *Great Books of the Western World* on many such lists. It was published in Basle in early 1536 (some say 1535). His intent was twofold, he writes in the introductory letter to King Francis I: (1) to justify the "Reformed" against unjust charges of civil rebellion, and (2) to help those coming new to the Bible at first-hand to grasp its basic lineaments.

Why had he decided to name his great treatise *The Institutes,* meaning the rudiments? Was that because he knew well the most enduring textbook ever published, Quintilian's vastly influential *Institutes of Oratory,* for fifteen centuries the foundation text to Western liberal arts education? He knew that the Roman rhetorician described his work as a "guide to the good man speaking." And that his secular prescription for making a person "good" was a reading program in the literature classic at the time of Quintilian's writing, just at the turn of the Christian Era.

Quintilian's view of oratory, much influenced by Cicero, was influential but not normative for Calvin's sermonizing. Olivier Millet meticulously demonstrates, in his extensive study *Calvin et la dynamique de la parole,* how Calvin drew widely upon the classical sources of rhetorical theory but governed his practice in ways uniquely his own. Millet is challenging and profoundly instructive.

Does he not appropriate Quintilian's title *Institutes* precisely to argue that it must be Christianity, not the classics, which can premise that "*good* man, speaking well"? He chooses the title *Institutes,* then (the evidence is not to hand, was Dr. Battles' reaction to this theory), to go Quintilian's powerful treatise one better, just as Christianity can employ the pagan classics, to which Calvin pays ample tribute, in refining the soul but invades them with substance, and pushes beyond them to lasting moral achievement both temporal and transcendental. Such at least we will suppose implicit in that title *Institutes.*

All this comes to mind as time and miles slowly pass.

He smiles a little as he reflects that being a hunted fugitive had hardly been the worst of his troubles. What a veritable maelstrom of them had tossed him wildly about in Geneva since Basle and his "little book," as he then called the *Institutes.*

And he recalls an abortive attempt to meet one Michael Servetus in Paris after he learned that this able young man might be won for Reform if only certain heretical notions of his about the Trinity were replaced with sound doctrine. He had proposed a rendezvous through a go-between, and in disguise entered Paris at some risk to his life. Servetus, also already condemned by the Inquisition to the shadow of the stake, did not show. They were to meet only after Servetus' misguided venture into Geneva some years later. But Calvin took the risk. Duty became a habit.

God chose failure and expulsion from Geneva as part of what Calvin, as we have noted, came to call his "early training." He learned that God set the pulpit at the head of the Church, and set the Church at the head of the City, with the sovereign God ruling in both by way of his inspired

Word projected into history by preachers ordained by Church and Spirit so to dare.

It's a burden an Erasmus never assumed, nor a Luther. For Calvin the Word addresses normatively — from the pulpit — both Church and state, both the personal and the societal. The shibboleth of "separation" never occupied his consciousness. Life forbids such artificial distinction. Indeed, Calvin's sense of Bible-induced civic responsibility became the hallmark of the Calvinist Puritanism that brought the democratic way of life to the West. The City is well and creatively "entrusted" to pulpits where a courageous ministry dares to "do all things in God's Word." *Then and only then, thus and only thus* ... as a Cromwell saw and said. Are there such pulpits today?

Calvin realized, as he rode along, that he had indeed enunciated in 1536 the formula for the *being* of the Church, coordinate with the *well-being* of the City: *Word preached!* This is God's creative instrument, and disciplinary "Sword of the Spirit" sheathed in the Holy Scriptures, drawn and brandished on the pulpit. . . . Had not — he thinks once more — God called the creation into Being with his Word? Had not Jesus, Son of God, stilled the raging sea, and retrieved Lazarus from the dead with the Word? And so healed the sick? And routed demons? Is not all Christianity from "in the beginning" to the final judgment borne into history by Word? Lived in history by way of Word incarnate in behavior? And that most effectively by way of Word *preached?*

He saw all too vividly how expulsion and exile were teaching him that somehow, somewhere Farel and he had muffed their challenge. The door to Geneva had been opened and God had indeed offered them access to founding a City. They had stepped in, but something had gone awry, and now *this!* Driven to Strasbourg. At first, "I confess, with pleasure unbecoming. . . ."

—⊶⊷—

His purpose at first with the *Institutes,* we have noted, had been twofold:
(1) to justify the Reform, and assure the King that those who adhered to
it were not the disloyal seditionists they were painted by the Catholic
prelates; they were simply Christian in ways the Church had neglected
to stress; and (2) to help those coming newly to the Faith to make their
way through the Bible. Meant to be just a little thing, really. Its success
surprised him. That others wanted to know what he, John Calvin,
thought: Why so? His intention had still been to do some "scholarly"
work. Yes, he mused, that *had been* his intention. But Geneva had
tainted, and would finally destroy, that aspiration.

Grimly he recalled that a treatise plays little active historical role out
of quiet retreat upon library shelves; its writer does not wrestle with, let
alone transform, the brutal forces that dominate what may be mistakenly called the city.

Those of the "gown," the intellectual elite who dabbled in the treatise and the lecture, were ever alien to the "town" that sheltered and sustained them. Only God, not scholarship however touted, can liberate
the selves and mold the wills that make the City. This Calvin knew almost from childhood. But now he is being shown by experience that
God's preference for that guidance, in battle with the Enemy, is pulpit
over lectern, is Word-preached over lecture, is *viva voce* over print, save
that print which embodies the divine Word. Yes, something normative
about that Genesis account of *"And God said ..."* gripped him more and
more. Preach, friend! For Calvin the "scholarly" life was becoming a
dream eclipsed by the vision of a revolutionary, City-forming Christianity, inevitable fruit of the Word falling from human lips ordained to the
task.

This was not the dominant vision of Luther nor Erasmus, nor of the
Vatican of the time, but the rootage of a far-reaching, new, "Reformed"
tradition.

Did the Lord, and did his world, need a second Erasmus? Another
Luther? Or was the Church to be carried on beyond the "personal ac-

quaintance with Jesus" into the communal experience long hoped for as the *civitas?* The answer is implicit in Calvin's developing perception of the civic creation implicit in preaching the Word.

Thinking once more of Geneva, he recalls very well how he had at first refused Farel's entreaties. Remembers vividly their quarrel. Sees now what Farel then saw, and what Calvin was yet unwilling to see, the self-indulgence hidden behind the facade of that "scholarship" on which Calvin was determined to expend, if not waste, his talents. Was not Erasmus, in point of fact, something of a pan-handler hovering ever so adroitly on the fringes of the Reform initiated by Brother Martin with his ninety-five theses? Is not, we may ask, the "scholar" always too likely to be so? Is not the adulation that "scholars" enjoy generally derived from among themselves? A customary exchange of academic back-scratching? Supported by the labor, but not to the benefit, of those who do the world's work? Calvin came clearly to see that. And in his Calvinism daily work achieved the understanding and appreciation so City-creating but so exploited by Marxist theory and corrupted by Marxist practice.

How much simpler, he mused, time passing silently by — and that not for the first time — to subdue Seneca's text to one's bidding than to subdue oneself and others to God's. Better and better he knew, with Erasmus ever slipping further from envy, that it was the Lord who enlisted him against every fiber of mind and body to take up the task of showing how effective is the Word in disciplining a mass, small or large, into a "City." We have already noted how aptly historian Émile Léonard profiles it: "Calvin invented a new kind of man in Geneva — Reformation man — and in him sketched out what was to become modern civilization" (I, 307). Quite other than offering free passes to glory.

And, when his Lutheran associate and dear friend Philipp Melanchthon declines to enter the lists of Quixotic pulpiteering windmill fighters, Calvin cannot escape admission of how frivolous a pretense at involvement masquerades as "scholarship," as his letters reveal. God designed that it will not be his course, nor that of the tradition he bequeathed to the world. Calvinists came to rank high among "doers," thinkers eager to have thoughts tested on the streets of the City at whatever risk to themselves.

Of course, as experience proved, God had uniquely qualified him for City-building, not out of his own resources *(this illusion is the grave defect of Marxism)* but as "minister" of the inspired Word. All that he had written of the Power of the Word on the lips of the faithful minister, long (it seemed) before he saw Geneva, that Word *will* accomplish, given an authentic vehicle for its proclamation and the cooperative role of the Holy Spirit — God's to choose when and where. That is the witness of Calvinist Puritanism.

Geneva obliges him to turn from vision of scholarly treatise to biblical commentary for the purpose of equipping a pulpit ministry to exert the Lord's rule by way of his Word faithfully expounded. He discovered that by the meticulous preaching of a biblical book, verse by verse, God would indeed accomplish his purposes. God knows the hour, sees the need, observes the opening, and fulfills the Prophet's prediction: "... My Word ... shall accomplish that which I purpose" (Isa. 55:11). *You preach. Leave the rest to Me.* Cromwell saw it. The Calvinist preacher lived it. God uses his Word as he chooses to accomplish all that he wills. Let the preacher but loose that Word into time and place. The Calvinist pulpiteer does not make himself triumphant in the remarkable accomplishments attributable to preaching. The faithful Calvinist preacher finds this Word doing all things that God chooses when he speaks it into history, vehicled by the syllables of his native tongue. So he comes to prescribe. In that he comes to rejoice.

He, Farel, and their few associates had foolishly thought to promote order by way of "Ecclesiastical Ordinances" (he reflected), adopted in early 1537 by the Council on their recommendation. Good idea, it

seemed at the time. Especially serving the Lord's Supper frequently so
that the ministers might examine all who partook of the elements as to
their conduct, with threat of excommunication in the background. An
idea borrowed no doubt from the Catholic confessional. They had
hoped much of that *method* of social control. They took it then as God's
way to discipline disciples and thus conform Geneva to the ancient vision of the City. Something of a crutch, was it, for the pulpit to lean
upon? Setting the inspired Word to doing whatever *they* had in mind?

Was that, perhaps, their mistake? he muses. To hope that a
"method," any method, would "convert" the anti-social to the social —
the "love of self," in Augustine's terms, into the "love of God"? Had they
under-estimated the inherent Power of the Word? Or of the Enemy?

True, they had multiplied Church services, but had they fully perceived the meaning of what Calvin was to call Christ's *ruling* by the
"scepter of his Word" preached? The sermon, he well knew, brings the
Word at first hand, as from God's lips to people's ears, the minister an
ambassador bearing a Light and Power not his own. Obedience to the
text obliges patient waiting upon what the Lord intends the text to accomplish — if and when it be truly preached! God-to-human; and
human-from-God. No structure, no formulae, no priesthood in between. The root of modern democracy.

Resistance all along had been stubborn and grew. Many, especially of
the older families, resented those "new presbyters." Their Bishop had
been ousted, and who were these? Tempers flared. Hatred fueled rage.
And the Council frowned on excommunication where Church mem-
bership and citizenship with right of suffrage intertwined. Did Farel
and "that Frenchman" — only, after all, *their* preachers — delude themselves into thinking **they** would decide who could vote, with their excommunication? Did they think themselves Bishops? Vicars of God,
maybe, endowed with some kind of inerrant authority?

He shivered, still re-living the savage scenes of the last Genevan

week-end. From some accounts, one infers that a notorious Libertine
had declared it was his intention to partake of the Supper in Calvin's St.
Peter's. Put up to it, probably, to bring things to a head? The Council
had endorsed his so doing. The ministers dissented with their claim to
keep the Table pure. The Council had stormed. The scene was chaotic,
voices raised, threats uttered. The man in question says he will come
with his armed retinue, if necessary, to secure his "right" to the Sacrament. In that case, Calvin hotly rejoins, there will just be no Sacrament
at all on April 21! And in *that* case, the Council replies, there will no services either on April 21! Meeting adjourned!

So matters had been left. But, at the usual hour on Sunday the 21st,
Calvin calmly ascends his pulpit, and preaches out of Romans as his
custom was, and ever remained, starting at the point where he had left
off in the previous sermon. (And it is at this point where he commences
preaching again upon his recall in 1541.) Rumors were abroad. The congregation was tense. There is no Sacrament. As Calvin descends the
pulpit steps, gendarmes appear to escort him home. The Council had
decreed! Let the Reformers be gone from the city in two days!

Oh, the hoots, the threats, the derision, the venom that accompanied
them out of the city. The wounds burn within him still. Beza recounts
that Calvin had said to those supporters who also were on hand, "Certainly, had I been in the service of men, this would have been a bad reward; but it is well that I have served Him, who never fails to repay His
servants whatever He has once promised" (19).

But he cannot, of course, shrug off the fact that they had failed. If
the Word be invincible, they had failed to provide the Word suitable expression, artful conveyance. So Aristotle had long ago explained in his
great *Rhetoric*. Every failure, he said, of Truth to persuade reflects the
weakness of its advocates. It was not a comforting thought.

Now, looking about, he observes how beautiful all is. Natural voices witnessing to him in whom we live, and move, and have our being. But why had he ever permitted himself to be side-tracked into City-building? (It was, he was slowly being driven to see, no side-track at all, but the main business of the Church.) How indeed had he been tempted into shouldering "that cross," as he described it when his friend Viret urged him later to return?

But something was coming into view that he was finally to see clearly in Strasbourg, as fruit of his hectic stay in Geneva gradually matured.

On the one hand, speaking the Word into the faces of servants of the demonic Adversary in the hurly-burly of civil life had been excruciatingly painful, at times almost unbearable. How vividly he had experienced the "danger" of a truly faithful pulpit. A "living death," he thought it. He had, indeed, felt obliged to lend his own most energetic efforts to involve God's Word in every aspect of Genevan life. He had been no stranger to City Hall, to working on the City walls, to facing problems in labor relations, in the schools, in local and inter-city politics. How strenuously he obliged himself to live the "involved" life.

But on the other hand, what of the life of "scholarship" that he had left home for Paris dreaming of? The life of Erasmus had been good to Erasmus, but what had it meant for the Geneva that had confronted Farel and him? Which scholarly tools would serve? Erasmus remains to this day delightful reading, mine for term papers, indeed, but is he more than only sophisticated surrogate for confrontation? Was his *Praise of Folly* more than ironic?

How many treatises could muzzle the Devil here and now, there and then? Calvin had wondered that very early in the chaos they strove to discipline into discipleship, in obedience to the Lord's "make disciples" by "teaching them to observe all that I have commanded you" (Matt. 28:20). What help in forming a City out of the cross-currents of chaotic self-interests is to be found in the Erasmus-types he had longed to emulate? Did "scholarship" devolve into questioning the Word, to emend and alter it, because that exercise is so much safer than preaching what the Book actually requires? Was his passion for seclusion focused upon welfare of Church or of self? Was "scholarship" like the fig tree in the Passion account, flourishing leaves without any fruit?

Oh yes, he well knew Erasmus' *Handbook of the Militant Christian,* with its twenty-five rules concerning "what it means to live the Christian life." But Geneva had faced him with a question that Erasmus did not seem to resolve, one that "scholarship" never has resolved. Write the rules, yes; easy enough, in endless versions. Bookshelves groan under them.

But how get such rules into common practice? How get them even considered as normative outside the classroom where the professor is safely enthroned? But, beyond the academy, how provide the rules effective formulation and compelling sanction? He had learned how Erasmus himself had hovered ever so adroitly on the fringes of the struggle set in motion by Luther's theses, pan-handling his way through life, some might have said. If this be *militance,* who fights the battles? Who gets bruised? Who "chirps safely on the sidelines," as he put it? Where was the "scholar" while Farel and he confronted their congregations, faced the Council, and were pelted on the streets? What use was that *Handbook* in avoiding a confrontation that for them led summarily into exile?

Already we read in a letter to friend Francis Daniel, out of Lausanne in October of 1536, his contemptuous characterization of the studious as those "idle bellies with you, who chirp together so sweetly in the shade" — the quiet and safety of non-involvement. It was a view that experience only crystallized as time and social tempest hastened him on. There is no evidence that he ever sought excuse, so ready to hand with his expulsion, to exchange the chaos of street and pulpit with the quiet of the study; or that he wanted to exchange the composition of the treatise, useful as he found it sometimes to be, for the hurly-burly of regular declaration of the Word from his pulpit, with correlative involvement in the civic life bustling all about him.

He is concerned that rickety railings on second-floor balconies might betray children; he worries that house fires might be kindled in winter through carelessness; he himself inspects and works on the defenses of the city; he inquires into the disposition of sewage; he pesters the Council for public works projects to employ the jobless; he supports the right of labor to organize.

The effect of the sermon must be interventionist, and he practiced his preaching. The Devil provided him enemies enough. But let us reflect, in passing, if Satanic foes are not aroused, is the guide to, and by, the ministry authentically God's Word?

Let the likes of Erasmus stand with us, he came to see, or recognize the pen for the facade it so readily can be. He comes to speaking of "scholarship" as laying the "frigid hand" of speculation upon the Scriptures. Of what use in really building the City?

Yes, Geneva had made its imprint upon him, had put his *Institutes* to the proof, as surely God intended. Who, he learned, benefits more than the scholar from "scholarship"? And upon what public "dole" does he in fact live in busy ease?

His Genevan debacle had alerted him to the sociological tests of a theology, to make consequences *the ultimate test of its soundness,* just as obedience to God's Law is the crucial evidence for "love" of God. Indeed, Geneva had begun his understanding that "doctrine" (as theology in action) is the effective tool of the pulpit just as "divinity" (as theology at rest) obscures the inconsequence of the lectern.

Yes, it became indubitable, with the ancient Western wisdom, that it indeed is the City that educates the young, for better or for worse. The basic resource of the good City is ever the Church, not the school. Schools at best discover, elicit and train the faculties of the soul. The character of a society is formed by, as it surfaces in, its cities, true or counterfeit. Moreover, the ancient humanist tradition held that there is intimate relation between moral virtue and the wisdom becoming incarnate in culture. Only the good become wise. Only the wise sinew the City into creative school for the young, and teach as their lives illustrate the ancient truism that what one *is* speaks so loudly as to drown out what one tries to say.

The moral character of the City is, therefore, of crucial importance. And key to civic moral character, Calvin had come to know, is the Christianity of the inspired Word with its role ever to hand in the sermon. He had yielded his scholarly aspirations to Farel's impassioned entreaties because instinctively he knew that. A potential City beckoned; duty had opened a door. He never really wished it otherwise, protest as he would its hardships. His *Institutes* would be re-crafted to focus Christianity upon civil order. His doctrine of civil order crowned his great treatise with the structure of the City.

And his experience had sharpened that ancient question: How is the true City brought to existence? The ablest thinkers had spent themselves, and wrote some of their greatest treatises, on what the true City is. *But how is the City attained?* Did the classical wisdom know? Do modern ideologies create "cities"?

But one element remained ambiguous as Calvin and Farel undertook the schooling of Geneva. Augustine had indeed profiled the Power that evokes the true City out of the factions so often at discord within city walls. He called it "love of God." That was surely the driving incentive, *but how implanted?* Yes, by the Spirit! Of course, but through what means? The Church since Augustine had sought to institutionalize that Power to achieve its civil ends. Prelates had taken on the authority and life-style of kings and princes, the Popes presuming themselves the very "Vicars of Christ." But almost inevitably, across the centuries, an abuse of power that challenged Reformation ensued.

Was there not a better Way?

He saw more and more succinctly that *closing the circle that makes the true City waited upon clothing divine Power with socially effective form.* For that he is driven to look to the Sermon. He sees it before he ever laid eyes on Geneva, where it is doubly, triply confirmed.

How must "love of God," the true end of humanity and dynamic of Cities, be evoked? That was the problem they had faced from the beginning, and one that the "Ecclesiastical Ordinances" failed to resolve. Nor had Erasmus and his kind been helpful.

How clearly he was beginning to see that the impulse to creative obedience must be called into being by a Word coming from outside and working within the human self. (An option Marx chose to replace with force!) And that impulse is to be led by the Light and nourished by the Power both conveyed by Word from above, designed to penetrate and function from within. God's Word, not a method, evokes and disciplines the City-forming will to obey.

The sermon is the key!

For the City, *it's Word-preached all the way.* Then and Now! So life, and God through life, taught him!

And, already as he moved on toward Strasbourg, Calvin knew the direction to be taken. He had accepted the traditional description of the Church as *mater fidelium,* Mother of Believers.

Ah, but is not the Church also *Mother of Cities,* here and now? Is that not what Farel and he had undertaken to show? And had they not neglected taking seriously enough — the thought made him quite uncomfortable — had they not neglected the full force of what he had been led by the Spirit to write (he became sure of that) in that 1536 issue of his *Institutes,* already rehearsed as he had ridden on his way: "do all things in the Word"?

Geneva, just because it was as harsh as it was, obliged him to take stock. And how vividly he was coming to understand that his failure there, his humiliating departure, bore but one witness, namely that the divinely prescribed Power for the transformation of a crowd of human beings into a City is the divine Word best employed in one way: *preached* plainly, bluntly, openly from the pulpit. Not the treatises of an Erasmus, nor the fashioning of "Ordinances," nor even his own *Institutes,* nor Lutheran evangelistic appeal completes the circle of ancient aspiration.

The City most nearly enters upon its long anticipation when the Word comes to reign there through a ministry that dares try "all things" by it (or him) Who calls into being the Kingdom that he rules.

But such daring is not a common commodity. How much easier to offer Jesus as "savior" than preach him as Lord. How popular the one and threatening the other. Had Farel and he preached a crusadist "gospel," opening heaven to a march forward, to a fixed prayer, to explosive emotional release, in lieu of obedience to the Word, who then would have demanded their expulsion? Yes, but what prophetic status would Geneva ever have provided the Western world?

Sermon and City, pulpit and progress, the living voice and the life of obedience, all infused with the vitality of the Holy Spirit by way of the Holy Book — living Word and living Spirit — these became the hallmarks of the Calvinist Puritanism that swept like a cleansing flame across Europe and colonial America, honoring Geneva as its spiritual capital.

Boot camp largely behind him, John Calvin rides on to the next phase of his maturation — pastoring the French-speaking church of Strasbourg, association with Johan Sturm, great pedagogue and devotee of Quintilian and Cicero, and with Martin Bucer, some think a kind of spiritual father to the still maturing Reformer.

And then?

Back to Geneva.

To Preach.

6. Reply to Sadoleto

Not without works yet not through works

— Calvin, *Institutes of the Christian Religion*

Calvin in exile is given occasion, in 1539, to sum up where he thinks he is, in doctrine and life, by one Jacobo Sadoleto, Cardinal of the Roman Catholic Church, then resident at Carpentras, not too far from Geneva. What became the famous exchange of letters between them calls attention to certain very fundamental issues in the life of Church and believer, then and now.

Aware of the expulsion of the Reformers from Geneva, the Cardinal writes, as custom permitted, on March 18, 1539, a letter to his "dear children" of Geneva, inviting them back to Mother Church. Calvin is persuaded to respond, out of exile in Strasbourg, in a letter sent on September 1, 1539. The letters are now published as *A Reformation Debate*. Custom was that such communications be read by messenger from house to house, or to the people in popular assembly.

The thrust of the Cardinal's shrewd appeal may be paraphrased: "Now, dear children, that you have so wisely freed yourselves from those heretical pests and blind, selfish guides, regain your senses and come home. *Mother Church will see you safely into glory.*"

In the Cardinal's language: "We all therefore believe in Christ in order that we may find salvation for our souls, i.e. life for ourselves: than

46

this there can be nothing more earnestly to be desired, no blessing more internal, more close and familiar to us. For in proportion to the love which each man bears to himself is his salvation dear to him; if it be neglected, what prize, pray, of equal value can possibly be acquired?" (Calvin, *Reformation Debate*, 34-35).

One may suppose that sentiments like these motivate crowds now drawn to evangelistic crusades, mega-churches, and cults of various kinds. With the significant exception that for the Cardinal salvation through the Church is not a momentary declaration of faith but a lifelong enterprise of obedience to formulae of various kinds. Calvin shares the principle, but dismisses the Roman Church's version of "good works."

Sadoleto writes: "This Church has regenerated us to God in Christ, both nourished and confirmed us, instructed us in what to think, what to believe, wherein to place our hope, and also taught us by what way we must tend toward heaven. We walk in this common faith of the Church; we retain her laws and precepts" (Calvin, *Reformation Debate*, 37).

Calvin dismisses the Catholic "way . . . toward heaven" as trivial mummery: ". . . the Papists call these good works, to fast upon a saint's eve, to eat no flesh upon Friday, to keep Lent, to serve He saints and She saints, to trot from altar to altar, from chapel to chapel, to cause masses to be sung, to go on pilgrimage, yea they have such a number of these pelfs, that no man can find neither head nor tail in them; the devil hath forged them so many laws and statutes that there is neither bottom nor bank" (*Sermons*, 2 Tim. 3:16-17).

No one in Geneva had risen in response to the Cardinal's challenge. Perhaps no one could. Sadoleto was a scholar of repute, urbane, suave, subtle, proffering an engaging formulation focused upon self-interest. One suspects that Calvin has a fondness for him.

Someone in Geneva thinks of Calvin. And in September, Calvin writes to Farel that one Sulzer, a minister of the Church in Berne, "had brought hither the epistle of Sadolet. I was not very much concerned about an answer to it, but our friends at length compelled me. At the present moment I am entirely occupied upon it. It will be a six days' work" (*Letters*, I, 151).

And he warmed to the task.

On reflection, the issue posed by Sadoleto was crucial. Not only the religious future of Geneva, but also the course of Reform itself hung in suspension upon the decision of the people whose City was to become, (as it did) if they held true, the Rome of the Reformation.

Was Sadoleto mistaken? Might it not be argued now, as evangelistic crusades are advertised, that indeed "there can be nothing more earnestly to be desired, no blessing more internal" than salvation for the soul? And, unlike the Cardinal's proposal, the Way is not through the Church but on some version of "the sawdust trail." After one of his "campaigns" (this one in Dallas) Billy Graham inadvertently exposed the emptiness of evangelical "campaigns" by claiming an "end-run around the Church."

How commonly it is asserted that the Church and her pulpits can have no higher goal than to "save souls" or to be "plucking brands from the eternal fires." It is also claimed that evangelistic campaigns can in effect issue free passes into heavenly mansions in exchange for "accepting Christ," done by the raising of a hand, a march forward, even the kneeling at a television screen. It's a burgeoning business at the expense of Truth and Church.

Calvin's response is brusque.

He dismisses the Cardinal's stress upon salvation of the soul, no doubt just as he would the appeals of crusade evangelism: "It is not a very sound theology to confine a man's thoughts so much to himself, and not to set before him, as the prime motive of his existence, zeal to illustrate the glory of God. For we are born first of all for God, and not for ourselves. . . . This zeal ought to exceed all thought and care for our own advantage. . . . It certainly is the part of the Christian man to ascend higher than merely to seek and secure the salvation of his own soul" (*Reformation Debate*, 58). *"Merely"* the soul? Yes, so he said. And "higher" than the soul's salvation? *Higher!* To build, say, the City!?

The issue raised by the Cardinal is as timely as tomorrow, as is Calvin's response. Involved here is the question: What is Christianity up to in the world?

Is Christianity here to open heaven's doors? Or to solidify the earthly City's walls? To give away the Christ for word or gesture, or to exploit the freedom gained to faith on Calvary for creating the City as the Lord's earthly Kingdom?

Both of them at odds with the Catholicism of their times, Calvinists and Lutherans discovered deep division between them. The Calvinists, seeing eternal destinies already settled in divine predestination, found "salvation" in the creation of the City. Lutherans disputed predestination and played faith off against works. Calvin's letters carry complaints of Lutheran "persecution" of his adherents, worse than that of the Catholics, he says. And writing in the year before his death to fellow Reformer Henri Bullinger in Zurich, he says: "I am carefully on the watch that Lutheranism gain no ground, nor be introduced into France. The best means, believe me, for checking that evil would be that the confession written by me in the name of the Prince of Condé and the other nobles should be published, by which Condé would pledge his good faith and reputation, and endeavor to draw over the German princes to our party" (*Letters*, IV, 322).

Calvin speaks of Lutheranism as "that evil." Luther was known to mix references to Calvin with references to the Devil.

In his *Kalvinismus und Luthertum,* German theologian Hans Leube points out that in the final edition of his *Loci,* Luther's associate Philipp Melanchthon says that "Only in Christ can man become holy, and therefore it is false to hinge sanctity upon an eternal decree." Calvin can only be most reluctantly persuaded, Leube adds, that "Melanchthon thinks differently than himself" (12), but increasingly Calvin has been unable to ignore the ugly gap between the Lutherans and his own adherents. The seventeenth century, to which most of Leube's study is devoted, develops the bitter division which resulted. It is a difference, commonly unrecognized, which still separates "accepting Christ" from Calvinism.

The Cardinal attacks the Reformers as catering to self-interest, seeking power, breathing pride, and hungering for the satisfaction of greed.

This is an apt characterization, Calvin replies, of "the Roman pontiff, with all the herd of pseudo-bishops who have seized the pastor's office like savage wolves" (*Reformation Debate,* 75). He sees Reform as liberating the Church from her clerical predators.

It is a description no less of self-appointed evangelists of all seasons, plying their self-serving trade, "hawking cheap grace on street corners, at cut-rate prices," as Dietrich Bonhoeffer was to put it (in *The Cost of Discipleship*), wherein *using* Christ as route to bliss is masqueraded as *serving* him.

But, Calvin says, all these clerical perks the Reformers had consciously laid aside in leaving Sadoleto's communion. Had he chosen to stay in the Cardinal's Church, "it would not have been difficult for me to reach the summit of my wishes, namely the enjoyment of literary ease" (*Reformation Debate*, 54). Look, he might have said, at Erasmus!

We Reformers, Calvin continues, reject your easy pass to heaven, and decline the material benefits that the Cardinal and those like him pilfered at their ease from the Church. "We counseled that as much should be distributed to ministers as might suffice for a frugal life befitting their order without luxurious superabundance, and that the rest should be dispensed according to the practice of the ancient Church" — that is, to the use of the poor. We "aimed only at promoting the kingdom of Christ by our poverty and insignificance" (56).

Altogether appropriate, now and always. The question opens: How do spokespeople for him who had "nowhere to lay his head" (Matt. 8:20), colleagues of the Paul who supported himself by making tents, acquire life-styles of the rich and powerful?

Calvin turns instructively to a common misconception:

> If you would attend to the true meaning of the term *justifying* in Scripture, you would have no difficulty. For it does not refer to a man's own righteousness, but to the mercy of God, which, contrary to the sinner's deserts, accepts a righteousness for him, and this by not imputing his unrighteousness. Our righteousness, I say, is that which is described by Paul (2 Cor. 5:19), that God has reconciled us to himself in Jesus Christ. The means is afterwards added: by not imputing sin. He demonstrates that it is by faith

only we become partakers of this blessing, when he says that the ministry of reconciliation is contained in the gospel (67).

Then he goes on:

But, it seems, injury is done to Christ if, under the pretense of his grace, good works are repudiated; for he came to render a people acceptable to God, zealous of good works. To the same effect are many similar passages which prove that Christ came in order that we, doing good works, might through him be accepted by God. This calumny which our opponents have perpetually in their mouths, that we take away the desire for well-doing from the Christian life by recommending gratuitous righteousness, is too frivolous to give us much concern. We deny that good works have any share in justification, but we claim full authority for them in the lives of the righteous (68).

Since, therefore, according to us Christ regenerates to a blessed life those whom he justifies and, rescuing them from the dominion of sin, hands them over to the dominion of righteousness, transforms them into the image of God, and trains them by his Spirit into obedience to his will, there is no ground to complain that by our doctrine lust is given free reign (68).

The point is clear and contemporary: *Justification* is unavailable through good works, but its correlative, *sanctification,* is unavailable without them. The issue is basic, and Luther's failure to emphasize it no doubt accounts for Calvin's growing disinclination to promote Lutheranism until he sets himself against it altogether. There is no contradiction, nor contrariety, between James and Paul, nor ground, either, therefore, though Calvin does not point it out here, for Luther's dismissal of the Epistle of St. James as "right strawy" stuff in teaching that "faith without works is dead" (cf. Davies, 33-36).

What, then, do the Reformers ask? That is, what does God ask of those to whom he grants citizenship in his Kingdom through faith in Christ?

The primary rudiments by which we are wont to train to piety those whom we wish to win as disciples of Christ, are these: not to frame any new worship of God for themselves at random and their own pleasure, but to know that the only legitimate worship is that which he himself approved from the beginning. For we maintain, what the sacred oracle declared, that obedience is more excellent than any sacrifice (1 Sam. 15:22). In short, we train them by every means to keep within the one rule of worship which they have received from his mouth, and bid farewell to all fictitious worship (69).

Do you wish, then, to attain righteousness in Christ? You must first possess Christ; but you cannot possess him without being made partaker in his sanctification, because he cannot be divided into pieces (1 Cor. 1:13). Since, therefore, it is solely by expending himself that the Lord gives us these benefits to enjoy, he bestows both of them at the same time, the one never without the other. Thus it is clear how true it is that we are justified not without works yet not through works, since in our sharing in Christ, which justifies us, sanctification is just as much included as righteousness (*Institutes*, III,16,1).

Then he turns to another crucial issue: The authority the Cardinal assumes for the Church must be countered by the authority of the biblical Word of God. The sermon, the Church, the Christian life all draw substance and strength from the Bible as foundation for Christianity and the Christian life. To demean the Bible is high priority for the Devil. To affirm its divine origin and infallible character has high priority in Geneva and the Calvinist world.

Calvin puts it graphically, as applicable tomorrow as in 1538:

Give me, not some unlearned man from among the people, but the rudest clown, and if he is to belong to the flock of God, he must be prepared for that warfare which He has ordained for all the godly. An armed enemy is at hand on the alert to engage — an enemy most skillful and unassailable by mortal strength; to resist him, with what guards must not that poor man be defended, with what weapons armed, if he is not to be instantly annihilated? Paul informs us (Eph. 6:17) that the only sword with which he can fight is the Word of the Lord. A soul, therefore, deprived of the Word of God, is given up unarmed to the Devil for destruction. Now, then, will not the first machination of the enemy be to wrest the sword from the soldier of Christ? And what method of wresting it, but to set him doubting whether it be the Word of the Lord that he is leaning upon, or the word of man? What will you do for this unhappy being? Will you bid him look round for learned men upon whom reclining he may take his rest? But the enemy will not leave him so much as a breathing time in this subterfuge. For when once he has driven him to lean upon men, he will keep urging and repeating his blows until he throws him over the precipice. Thus he must either be easily overthrown, or he must forsake man, and look directly to God. So true it is that the Christian faith must not be founded on human testimony, not propped up by doubtful opinion, not reclined on human authority, but engraven on our hearts by the finger of the living God, so as not to be obliterated by any coloring of error (*Reformation Debate,* 78-79).

How vividly Calvin profiles the encroachment upon faith of the unbelief so characteristic of the mind of modernity, indeed the mind of the so-called scholarly "cutting-edge" in all modernities, arrogantly flouting what it has never been given really to know. How perceptively Calvin foresaw unceasing attack upon Christianity by way of demeaning the Bible:

Now, then, will not the first machination of the enemy be to wrest the sword from the soldier of Christ? And what method of wresting it, but to set him doubting whether it be the Word of the Lord that he is leaning upon, or the word of man?

Precisely so! Ever so across the ages! Never more true of an age than of our own, when desperate efforts are constantly mounted to exclude the Bible from every institution where unbelief finds a toehold.

A popular Darwinism, which explains nothing, really, of human origins, runs cover for rejection of the biblical Genesis, and thus of the authority of the Bible altogether. It has long been so; will long be.

"Now . . . will not the first machination of the enemy . . . ?" Yes, of course!

And John Calvin, then and for always: **"So true it is that the Christian faith must not be founded on human testimony, nor propped up by doubtful opinion, nor reclined on human authority, but engraven on our hearts by the finger of the living God, so as not to be obliterated by any coloring of error."**

And here we can discern the over-riding goal drawing him back to Geneva and binding him to the pulpit of his St. Peter's: the extension of the "kingdom of Christ" by the application of his "scepter" — the Word — to the City of Geneva, and indeed to all potential Cities everywhere. Many still to go, even now!

Was it, is it, Quixotic? A chaotic populace, a pulpit, a Word — and out of that a "Kingdom" in Geneva? In Europe? Across the sea? Around the world? All by way of Word off pulpit?

Quixotic? Yes, from some points of view. Never lacking. Ever noisy.

But sober reality, if God be God, Word be true, and vision borne by faith vibrantly alive.

That is the indubitable witness of Calvinist Puritanism across Western history.

We might observe, as revealing in passing, a striking judgment Calvin includes in his letter reflecting on the form of the Cardinal's subtle appeal to self-interest in the name of the Church. It comes, Calvin avers, *"in poor taste"!*

We've already noted that Barth and others do speak of Calvin as the "aristocrat" among the Reformers. He is sensitive to "good taste," this generally neglected facet of sanctity, bad theology *sinning* by betraying an absence of sensitivity to God's appropriate. Calvin, the aristocrat, is sensitive to it.

By birth and preference, Calvin is repelled by pell-mell pursuit of heavenly bliss, blinded to the needs of the hour, indifferent to the City, eye fixed upon self-satisfaction, which betrays Christianity by "poor taste"! Calvin is keenly aware, as Charles Williams emphasizes in his remarkable study of Dante, *The Figure of Beatrice,* that Christianity dwells among humankind as enculturating source of good manners, of quiet elegance, measured in *noblesse oblige,* the social environment of the true City, promoted by Christian love and precisely the antipodes of life as portrayed in Dante's *Inferno* and its grim contemporary historical counterparts.

For Calvin says, "Therefore if we would know whether a man have profited well in the Gospel or not, let us mark his life" (*Sermons,* 2 Tim. 3:16-17). Has the Word taken possession? It will show. Does the "Christian" validate faith by constructing the City? Also by way of a sense of style and courtesy? Here, in the case of the learned Cardinal from whom good taste is to be expected?

"I take it for granted," he says in his *Institutes,* "that there is such life energy in God's Word that it quickens the souls of all in whom God grants participation in it. . . . I mean that special mode which both illumines the souls of the pious into the knowledge of God and, in a sense, joins them to him. Adam, Abel, Noah, Abraham, and other patriarchs cleaved to God by such illumination of the Word" (II,10,7). And it glowed in their behavior!

Of himself and colleagues in the ministry, he says, ". . . We must live an holy life; the Gospel is not to teach us to talk, it is not to make us eloquent and subtle, and I know not what; but it is to reform our lives, that the world may know our desire to serve God, to give ourselves wholly to him, and to conform ourselves to his good will."

So much for the ministry; and then for all: "Therefore if we would know whether a man have profited well in the Gospel or not, let us mark his life. Truth it is that a number may leap high enough, and again, they may have tongue at will, and yet if we find not such agreement in their life to the justice of God, as S. Paul requires, we know that all the rest of their life is naught because it is not framed after the Gospel as it ought to be" (*Sermons,* 2 Tim. 3:16-17).

7. Out of Exile . . . Geneva Again

Expulsion from Geneva did not turn out to be the full liberation that Calvin anticipated. He sensed that, even as he was leaving Geneva. He applied almost at once for permission to return. Rejected. But did he not sense still being divinely chosen to endure the terrible struggles of blazing the path from riotous Geneva to a City?

In that spring of 1538, the time of "training" seemed over. Oh, great joy! Calvin was out. Geneva had lifted from his shoulders the intolerable burden . . . of Geneva. Leisure for scholarly publication was just around the corner of the road to Strasbourg. Means sufficient for existence, even when on occasion he must sell a precious manuscript, were to hand. Why, then, was he not at ease shepherding the French church of Strasbourg?

The God who "commandeered" him kept John Calvin on short leash. No Calvin, and no Calvinist, ever took lightly failure to fulfill commitment. Conscience, sternest of masters, never let go. Geneva had been "entrusted" to his care, not by the Genevans but by the God of the Genevans, known or unbeknownst to them. We know that Marx suffered also the sacrifices wrought by conscience. He writes in one of his letters of the self-denials imposed upon him and those he loved by his absorption in "duty" to the oppressed. What if, we may reflect, the nineteenth-century Church had been true enough to Calvin to challenge that flaming ideologist Marx with the Word, promoting the kind of social justice (in lieu of "Are you saved, brother?") that Geneva found mandated by the true pulpit, not by the crusade, nor the treatise, nor sweet "scholarly" chirping in the shade of inconsequence? Might the Marxist ideology have failed to convulse the course of history?

Resolving the wrenching choice between recall to Geneva and continued sojourn in Strasbourg was always in either the forefront or background of Calvin's mind, we may infer, from the first step into Strasbourg. Here came to the surface the alternatives, scholarship after the order of Erasmus, with all its attractions, or civic involvement inspired by the Word of God as mirrored in the lives of those inspired by Calvin courageously to refashion Europe and the colonial United States by taking all the risks of obedience.

Calvin's correspondence breathes the terrible struggle between the attractive life of "scholarship" and that of desperate involvement. For the slow, painful "conversion" God imposed upon him there was no sawdust trail, no accepting guarantee of heaven for the wave of the hand, no giving faith away or "sharing Christ" in ease and convenience. It was pleasant in Strasbourg. The company was good: Bucer in theology, Sturm in culture and education, and others passing by. The illusion of doing God's work in the world from the lectern, at the desk, and by way of the colloquy was tempting. Works could in no way earn justification. Was not Heaven free for the taking?

Or was it?

Justification is free, but only as correlative to a sanctification without which there is no salvation. What Luther had rejected as a "right strawy epistle" teaches that "faith without works is . . . dead" (James 2:26). "All right knowledge of God," Calvin says, "is born of obedience" (*Institutes* I,6,2).

The life of obedience for him, only interrupted by expulsion, still led through Geneva and St. Peter's pulpit. It was cross-bearing all the way. This he knew as he lived out the "leisure" of Strasbourg, while both from within and from outside the tug of Geneva made itself more and more imperative.

At least some of the letters coming to and going from Strasbourg are available. They reflect the intensity of choice confronting a gifted man when duty and inclination clash, when the hand of God is not quite hidden in events that conspire to point beyond convenience.

Making a City of Geneva was interrupted business. Calvin could not endure commitment unfulfilled. His letters reflect the intense tussle between duty and desire.

He decides, finally, to ask for, and accept, the advice of close friends. He writes to Farel,

> For I much prefer to be entirely blind, that I may suffer myself to be guided by others, than to go astray by trusting my own pur-blindness. If, in these circumstances, I shall ask your advice as to whose judgment I ought chiefly to defer to, you will reply, if I am not mistaken, that there are none more proper to be consulted than *Capito* and *Bucer*. What they think upon it you have heard from themselves. I wish you would explain the whole case fully to the brethren, and that divesting themselves of prejudice on either side, they would seriously consider what ought to be done. This is the sum of the whole: that I am not in this affair actuated by craft or cunning — the Lord is my witness; neither do I search about for loopholes whereby to make my escape. Certainly, indeed, it is my desire that the Church of Geneva may not be left destitute; therefore, I would rather venture my life a hundred times over than betray her by my desertion. But forasmuch as my mind does not induce me spontaneously to return, I am ready to follow those who, there is some good hope, will prove safe and trusty guides to me (*Letters*, I, 213).

And then he writes again to Farel, in August, 1541, who as expected is joined by the others to counsel return:

> As to my intended course of proceeding, this is my present feel-ing: had I the choice at my own disposal, nothing would be less agreeable to me than to follow your advice. But when I remember that I am not my own, I offer up my heart, presented as a sacrifice to the Lord [this was the substance of the famous emblem which Calvin adopted for himself]. Therefore I submit my will and my affections, subdued and held fast, to the obedience of God; and

whenever I am at a loss for counsel of my own, I submit myself to those by whom I hope the Lord himself will speak to me (*Letters*, I, 280-81).

He writes to the Seigneury of Geneva on September 7, 1541, that he is on his way, going through Berne to meet with the Council and ministry there.

And then he writes to Farel from Geneva on September 16, 1541, almost laconically, in the quiet after the storm: "As you wished, I am settled here; may the Lord overrule it for good" (*Letters*, I, 284).

John Calvin returned to Geneva on September 13, 1541, his exile over. The *Registre* of the Council records his appearance before them and their promise to proceed immediately with the creation and adoption of new "ecclesiastical ordinances," to which end a committee of six was appointed to join Calvin. He was assigned an annual stipend of "five hundred florins, twelve measures of corn, and two tuns of wine." For a dwelling they offered him "the mansion *Fragneville* with an ell of velvet for clothing" (*Letters*, I, 284).

The intensity of the struggle was the measure of the man. He was back.

The Sermon

But do all things in God's Word!

— Calvin, *Institutes*

8. Perspective: *The Institutes*

No accomplished writer, least of all a John Calvin, puts his hand to a literary project without clear view of the end from the beginning.

When he took up his pen to begin work on his *Institutes of the Christian Religion,* he knew what Christianity is in the world for. If Christ had suffered and died only to guarantee the soul's salvation, Calvin might have focused his book on the doctrine of predestination enunciated almost in passing in 1535. Or he might have shelved his pen and commended Lutheranism.

If the intent of the *Institutes* had been to push on from sound doctrine to the character of the obedient life, the treatise could have ended with the conclusion of Book Three. And in fact, since 1550 its chapters 6-10 have been occasionally published separately in a variety of languages as *Calvin's Golden Booklet of the Christian Life.*

But, Calvin did not stop there and had no intention of doing so. His mind set on that we have already observed as revealed in the letter to Sadoleto: "It certainly is the part of the Christian man to ascend higher than merely to seek and secure the salvation of his own soul" (*Reformation Debate,* 58).

And as he also wrote: "Do we want, then, as I have said, to profit in the school of our God, so that his teaching may be useful to us and we may be edified by it? Let us always have this foundation — it is that we try to devote ourselves to the obedience of our God, that he may be exalted in the midst of us, that he may have the reverence he

63

deserves. When this happens, we shall be building well" (*Sermons,* 1 Tim. 4:7).

And key to such "building well," then?

That perspective emerges in Book Four.

While Calvin's structuring of the *Institutes* underwent rearrangement, as meticulously traced out by Ford Battles in his *Analysis of the Institutes of the Christian Religion,* and though the substance enjoyed progressive enhancement from the first edition of 1536 through the last of 1559, the essential content, and intent, was there from the first: Christianity is in the world to qualify those who believe to find goal and meaning in the kind of life which creates the *City,* long foreseen by those gifted to envision the day after tomorrow, and in the course of more recent centuries given drive, emphasis, and content through the Calvinist church.

Students of Calvin seem to agree that his convictions really never underwent essential change. He early knew who he was and where he wanted to go, and he went there with least expenditure of space and energy. And from that first evening with Farel, Calvin must have sensed that Geneva was stuff provided by God to give substance, and trial, to the insights that the Bible gave his *Institutes.* It was, as he said, "all in the Word." No one was more certain, risked more, and gave more for that conviction.

In its final edition, the *Institutes* appears in four Books:

Book One: The Knowledge of God the Creator
Book Two: The Knowledge of God the Redeemer in Christ
Book Three: The Way in Which We Receive the Grace of Christ
Book Four: The External Means or Aids by Which God Invites
             Us into the Society of Christ and Holds Us Therein

In sum: If the intent of the *Institutes* were exposition of the Apostles' Creed, prompted by the neglect of "sound doctrine" then prevailing in the Church, Calvin need not have designed to go beyond the first half or so of Book Three.

But, if Calvin be uniquely convinced that — with eternal destinies settled from before the creation — Christianity comes to complete in history, so far as fallen humankind can be redeemed to it, the view of the good life embodied in the ancient dream of the City given the wisest and best, then Book Four substantiates the intention implicit from the beginning.

Here, in Book Four, he sketches two ideas: (1) the form of civil government commended in Scripture and competent to structure the City, and (2) the kind of preaching designed in revelation to achieve such government.

Professor Battles implies as much in his *Analysis:*

> *The Institutes of the Christian Religion* is a bold effort to crown God as King of His people (3.20.45). That God may rule among the nations — is this not the central theme of Calvin's theology? Calvin never speaks literally of the "sovereignty of God," a pale abstraction that cuts away the essential biblical, royal imagery. This explains the "political frame" of the *Institutes:* it begins with the letter to the French King, Francis I, and ends with the famous chapter on *political* government (4:20). Calvin's theology lives in the real world and squarely faces it. Calvin's career as writer and leader was not that of a utopian dreamer or theorist; for him the study of law and theology meet at the deepest level (18).

This is a bold stroke made against the prevailing stream of Calvin studies by one who was as prudent as he was highly gifted.

And we may remind ourselves here of Ernst Troeltsch's exuberant approbation:

> Indeed, the great importance of the Calvinistic social theory does not consist merely in the fact that it is one great type of Christian social doctrine; its significance is due to the fact that it is one of the great types of sociological thought in general. In inner significance and historical power the types of French optimistic equalitarian democracy, of State Socialism, of totalitarian Communist Socialism, and of the mere theory of power, are, in comparison with Calvinism, far behind (II, 622).

We may say, then, that for John Calvin the Church is in the world to create the social structure long called *City*, with the *Institutes* leading the way. It's why he did become a "world power." The Calvinist/Puritan mind saw that with remarkable clarity, as illustrated in those who settled the New World: "As Winthrop and other guiding spirits conceived it, they were embarked upon a special errand, or mission, for their Maker. . . . They were to try to construct a model community. . . . As Winthrop put it, 'Wee shall be as a City upon a Hill, the eyes of all people are upon us'" (Catton and Catton, 93-94). As precisely in the spirit of Book Four as were the sentiments of Cromwell, already noted.

For John Calvin, Jesus came to live, to die, and to rise again to take rule in human history as King, for the creation through the Word declared by the Church through her pulpits, of "a model community" we've been calling "City" and the "Kingdom," which is illustrated in the world of the West.

9. Way-Station: The Christian Life

The obedient Christian life that blossoms into the City is concisely profiled by Calvin in Book Three of *The Institutes,* chapters 6 to 10. His summary catches the flavor of the whole, not only of the treatise but of John Calvin himself:

> We are not our own: let not our reason nor our will, therefore, sway our plans and deeds.
>
> We are not our own: let us therefore not set as our goal to seek what is expedient for us according to the flesh.
>
> We are not our own: in so far as we can, let us therefore forget ourselves and all that is ours.
>
> Conversely, we are God's: let us therefore live for him and die for him.
>
> We are God's: let his wisdom and will therefore rule all our actions.
>
> We are God's: let all the parts of our life accordingly strive toward him as our only lawful goal.
>
> O, how much has that man profited who, having been taught that he is not his own, has taken away dominion and rule from his own reason that he may yield it to God" (*Institutes* III,7,1).

Here is summarized the crucial difference between the two "loves"

67

that distinguish the two "Cities" profiled by Augustine, the love of God and the love of self.

Could there be a more succinct summation of *why* the Church, *why* the pulpit, and *why* the sermon? And *how* the City?

It would be difficult to phrase the underlying thrust of the Christian life more comprehensively.

Yet, challenging as are the ethical demands of Book Three, Calvin certainly was looking through these to the *socio-political* dimensions of the Gospel, a view culminating in his Book Four.

10. The Genevan Pulpit

If the pulpit's the thing, what do we know of preaching in Calvin's Geneva? There are the usual differences of opinion, as well as things to note. There was the ultimate lodging of authority in the Council. Civil government functioned in a variety of forms and officials. Calvin was influential as person and as pastor, but he was hardly a dictator.

Involved were the three major churches, Calvin's St. Pierre [Peter], St. Gervais, and La Madeleine. There were smaller congregations in outlying villages, and the preaching staff varied from as few as five to as many as eighteen, some traveling personally to represent from time to time Calvin's own relations with the capitals of Europe.

Calvin accompanied his preaching with regular lectures on the text of Scripture in the Auditorium; these became his Commentaries and cover most of the biblical books. These may be compared with his sermons on the same texts for flavor and focus.

The ministerial staff met regularly on Friday afternoons for discussion of on-going matters, and usually a textual exposition, called the "Congregation," often given by Calvin. Some of these have been preserved and published.

Writes Dartmouth professor Herbert D. Foster: ". . . in Geneva, five sermons on the pure Word of God on Sunday and two on each week day, with the 'hours so distributed that one may easily attend all, the one after the other' — a Puritan total of seventeen possible sermons a week!" (74).

Of Calvin himself, T. H. L. Parker says: "Calvin restricted himself to the two Sunday sermons and every day of alternate weeks, or rather, that was his general pattern of preaching. Sometimes, as on Deuteronomy, he preached from Monday to Friday of alternate weeks with an additional sermon on the intervening Wednesday. The Sunday sermons seem to have been given in St. Pierre, but those on weekdays were sometimes given in one of the other churches" (62).

Beza describes the preaching thus: "In every fortnight he preached one whole week; thrice every week he delivered lectures; on the Thursdays he presided in the meetings of the Presbytery; on the Fridays he collated and expounded the Holy Scriptures to what we term the congregation" (27).

Whatever was precisely the case, Calvin's emphasis upon the priority of sermonizing is certainly witnessed by his own allocation of limited time and energies to his St. Peter's pulpit.

It is sometimes said that church attendance was mandatory, but that seems unlikely. Strongly urged, carefully watched, no doubt of that. But, Calvin can refer from the pulpit to those who may or may not be present but ought to (not must?) be there.

We can hear, as typical, what Calvin said in the spring of 1555, when things seemed to be at an ebb that set him, so to say, packing his bags for another expulsion (that not for the first time after his return from exile). With the annual election-time — widely noted in Genevan and Calvinist/Puritan preaching everywhere — close to hand (which in fact was unexpectedly to give his followers a Council majority), Calvin preaching out of 1 Timothy, says of some candidates for office:

> Now, I ask you, how are they behaving in the election? For I need not wait to say something that is all too plain. When it is a question of electing and choosing the magistrates, they ought to be here to call upon the name of God, that he would preside at the Council and that he would give them a spirit of guidance and right. But where will they be? In the tavern, or at play. And those who have a vote are the least frequenters of sermons.

He goes on,

I have just met some of those louts, that I could point the finger at
— but there is no need; they are known well enough. . . . it seemed
to them that they would have no leisure for breakfast unless they
chose service time. I saw that with my own eyes as I came to
church. And is it not a quite notorious shame? (Parker, 123).

They appointed him. They paid him. He did not hesitate to make
preaching a "dangerous" affair.

We pass by as well enough known the abortive revolutionary attempt by a few in May, 1555, settled finally by execution and exile. And
the notorious Servetus matter, in October, 1553, certainly instanced often enough, and well described in Roland Bainton's *Hunted Heretic*.
These were only more conspicuous examples of the turmoil always implicit in Calvin's pulpitry, ameliorated in the turn of support found for
him in the shift occasioned by admission in 1555 of more French refu-
gees to the ballot. The story of these matters appears in many accounts,
well done in *The History and Character of Calvinism* by John T. McNeill
and carefully traced in Beza's *Life*.

The Pastor of St. Peter's held his course, come fair weather or foul.

11. The "City" — Civil Government

An attractive vision of sound, biblically disciplined civil government gleams at the apex of the *Institutes*. One detects in it the "City" of Calvin's heart, at which he believes the Word of God takes aim in pulpit and sermon. He combines the vision of the classical tradition with invigoration from the Word of God, quite the antithesis of "separation" of Church and State. His prophetic anticipation, waiting now upon further fulfillment, was of a fallen humankind reaching high for the challenge of the City by way of the Gospel. His anticipation finds substance and definition in what Christianity was sent, as he saw it, to do in history. As consciously revolutionary Agent (Trotsky saw it well), Calvin preaches the Word indefatigably to enlist the Light and Power of God in the creation of all that had so long been foreseen as the *Civitas* goal for humankind. Why else, with predestination assumed, mount the pulpit?

Indeed, the Word pointed the elect to obedient fulfillment of their destiny in ways not altogether foreign to Pericles, Plato, Aristotle, and Cicero.

There is something of the inevitable in Calvin's culminating the Christian life in the Christian democratic community. The tribute he pays in what I call his "Ode" to the sermon certainly implies the goal of preaching as creation of the life of responsible freedom guaranteed by the *City*. And almost naturally he caps Book Four with a quite remarkable tribute to the constructive, indeed indispensable, role of civil order in earth-bound human affairs. Editor McNeill appends a lengthy foot-

72

note to this concluding section, to stress that "Calvin turns here with startling abruptness to approve, and solemnly urge, action by a constituted magistracy to protect the liberties of the people" (*Institutes,* IV,20,31,n.54).

Calvin is revolutionary because Christianity can so impact human history. He assumed what the Church had yet to stress — and Marx never seriously did — that the "new society" is totally dependent upon creation, first, of a "new man," absolutely requisite to a "new," rather than merely "novel," order. That constitutes the import of Books One through Three of the *Institutes.*

Interestingly, Marx also went on record as recognizing the requirement of the "new" man if the old order is to be converted. In a supper speech at the Bell Hotel, Strand, published in *The People's Paper* of April 19, 1856, Marx says, "We know that if the newfangled forces of society are to work satisfactorily, they need only be mastered by newfangled men. . . " (Adorastskii, 91).

Ah, then Karl Marx *knew* that. How well a son of Abraham should have known it! How much the essence of a biblical approach to history!

And the issue has ever the more starkly emerged: *How* are the "newfangled men," so absolutely requisite to the City, to be obtained? It is a religious question, reminiscent of that alternative posed to Israel (as Marx well knew) by Moses, who confronted a liberated people then, as the Word still does a humankind liberated at Calvary, with a second rendition (*Deuter*onomy) of the divine Law of New Life. It echoes out of the long history of Israel, resounded over and again upon the pulpits of Calvinism: "Love . . . **that is obey** . . . God! For this very purpose he has, in Christ, set you — all of you — (Calvin was sure of that) free!" The very root of the City!

But Marx, who had early declared, "In short, I hate all gods!" preferred playing with whimsy to confronting reality — as do many self-anointed "realists." His talk goes on thus concerning the newfangled forms of society: "They need only be mastered by newfangled men, and such are the working men. They are as much the invention of modern time as machinery itself" (Adorastskii, 91).

Oh, clever blindness! Oh, fatal whimsy! Genius that he was, cute as is his offhand correlation of new machine = new man, Marx missed the very point he was making, and plunged the world into endless misery by licensing the brutal tyranny that Christianity restrained. The "new-fangled" person is indeed indispensable to funding creative change but never emerges full-blown from change itself. The preacher who speaks not first to himself serves no one. Marx's easy, and indeed whimsical, specification of "new" people as natural offspring of "new" machinery may be, perhaps, misconceived as implicit in his dialecticism, but the equation has proved to be lethally unrealistic. It's not that natural, as Marx himself might well have discerned from his aborted efforts to evoke an "International" out of the working-class eruptions his ideology so brilliantly stimulated . . . and defrauded.

Institutes editor McNeill appends here a quotation from Calvin's commentary on Daniel 6:22: "For earthly princes lay aside their power when they rise up against God, and are unworthy to be reckoned among the number of mankind. We ought, rather, utterly to defy them [*conspuere in ipsorum capita*, lit., 'to spit on their heads'] than to obey them" (IV,20,31,n.54).

Here, then, is what Calvin believed — even before coming to Geneva — that God designs a Word-created *civil government* to be and to do. This is, it seems to me, the vision that guided what he and Calvinism sought to accomplish, primarily by way of the sermon — and largely did.

Here's his accolade to the civil government he believes that the Church must pursue: (Now there's a goal for a crusade evangel: Preach this "calling"!)

Its function among men is no less than that of bread, water, sun and air; indeed, its place of honor is far more excellent. For it does not merely see to it, as all these serve to do, that men breathe, eat, drink, and are kept warm, even though it surely embraces all these activities when it provides for their living together. It does not, I repeat, look to this only, but also prevents idolatry, sacrilege against God's name, blasphemies against his truth, and other public offenses against religion from arising and spreading among the people; it prevents public peace from being disturbed; it provides that each man may keep his property safe and sound; that men may carry on blameless intercourse among themselves; that honesty and modesty may be preserved among men. . . . No one ought to doubt that civil authority is a calling, not only holy and lawful before God, but also the most sacred and by far most honorable of all callings in the whole life of mortal man. (*Institutes,* IV,20,3-4)

Was this the vision before his mind's eye as he mounted, month by month and year by year, his St. Peter's pulpit?

While preferences vary, does in fact Jean-Jacques Rousseau, who was well aware of having been born into a Geneva once dominated by Calvin, pen as tempting a view of civil order in his *Social Contract?*

Obviously, the so-called "separation" of Church and State is a shibboleth quite foreign to Calvin and recklessly inimical to humankind. Calvin takes note of that in opening his discussion of civil government: "For although this topic seems by nature alien to the spiritual doctrine of faith I have undertaken to discuss, what follows will show that I am right in joining them, in fact, that necessity compels me to do so" (*Institutes,* IV,22,1). A "necessity" that exacts heavy toll of those who follow the prating of "separation" in our own times.

He adds, "The Lord not only testified that the office of magistrate is approved by and acceptable to him, but he also sets out its dignity with most honorable titles and marvelously commends it to us" (*Institutes,* IV,22,4). Where is the pulpit enunciating *this* today?

Calvin stubbornly baptizes the best of the Western hope. He promotes a happy and constructive common purpose uniting the biblical role assigned civil government with the ancient Western vision of the "City." His preparation for comment on the *De Clementia* obliged him to explore ancient political theory and the great theorists of the Western mind. His *Institutes* focuses the Gospel upon historical realization of the wisdom that an over-arching Providence revealed to Western foresight.

12. The Means: "Ode" to the Sermon

And so, as Calvin indeed sees the classic vision of the City as prophetic, and finds in Scripture a profile of the kind of civil government that promises attainment of that vision, he comes firmly to declare that God provides humankind his Word for preaching such government, and thus the City, into existence. Surely it is with this view in mind that he undertakes to preach his way through the entire Bible. Unleash the Word; leave with God the rest, including the City.

In practical terms, we can draw the equation ourselves. We have already taken note of both elements: (1) Geneva before and (2) Geneva after exposure to Calvin's pulpit influence. That is, (1) Geneva unruly and chaotic, and (2) Geneva thought by some a miracle of civil order.

With what, he might point out, in between?

For the believer, the obvious answer is: with biblical preaching in between. His kind of preaching, which he characterized in what I call his "Ode" to the sermon. That was the dynamic cause of the "new" Geneva.

If, however, you are inclined to unbelieving that sermons can be cures for civil disorder, thinking Calvin mistaken and his performance of his own convictions unconvincing, there are other options for explaining the "new" Geneva, many of them tried out across the years. Certainly the most formidable among them are the ideologies. Geneva registered her record; ideologies have created theirs — Communism, Fascism, Nazism, Muslim *jihad,* and other forms of the totalitarian. (In what blindness is ideology preferred by so many?)

It seems likely that Calvin views preaching, one comes to believe, in the Light of the astonishing Power of the "And God said . . . " of Genesis. God speaks; so it is! St. John confirmed that the creative Word Who speaks all things into being is the Christ of God.

That this creative Power can be tapped by the Church to the benefit of humankind is why God presents it in the form of Word, fitted to the mysterious power of speech.

God's Word comes to all upon the pages of Holy Scripture, incarnate in the language there prevailing. The sermon is the divinely prescribed manner of broadcasting that Word into time, world, and history. It is God's way of getting his will incarnate in human behavior.

The text, preached, will reveal complementary realities: (1) what God says, (2) what God means, and (3) behavior correlative to these.

Meaning can take expression in many verbal forms, correlative to the sensitivity, the learning, the experience, the vision, and the intention of the preacher. Meaning, for Calvin, lays hold of listener performance: intellectual, emotional, volitional. "All right knowledge of God," we recall his saying, "is born of obedience" (*Institutes*, I,6,2).

The goal of the ordained preacher is to bring God's Word to incarnation in human behavior resulting in creation of the City, and maturation of the soul. This is what he means by *preaching!* And what he arduously seeks to illustrate.

The extraordinary accomplishments Calvin attributes to the Word, in no other manner accessible to humankind, account for his predilection for preaching. The "Ode" exhibits why a theologian so learned, a writer so gifted, spends so much of his allotted time and limited energies in his St. Peter's pulpit, insisting upon being carried up to it in the chair even now on display there, even when physically handicapped by recurrent illnesses. He is preaching a Word chosen by God, inspired by God, to convey God himself into time, space, and City.

We must keep clearly in mind that the "Word" Calvin is here eulogizing is incarnate in that Bible so quietly glowing on our shelves, our tables, at our bedsides. And we might well remember his conviction that handling the divine Word is always superintended by angels.

"But where is the Word of God to be found, unless we see it in the

Law, and in the Prophets, and in the Gospel? For there it is that God has set forth his mind to us" (*Sermons*, 2 Tim. 3:16).

If you come to believe that there is indeed a "sovereign power" capable of doing all that is instanced in the "Ode" (patience!) and available to those able to use that Word as God intends, what other Power would, or could, or *should* be preferred? And would it not be obvious that an institution authorized to train, ordain, and support those appointed to proclaim that Word is unique among all others in the world, as the Church of Jesus Christ?

Is that not why so many churches have tall steeples, lightning-rod conductors of the fire of Speech out of heaven?

This is his "Ode" (that name is not his):

> Here, then, is the sovereign power with which the pastors of the church, by whatever name they be called, ought to be endowed. That is that they may dare boldly to do all things by God's Word; may compel all worldly power, glory, wisdom, and exaltation to yield to and obey his majesty; supported by his power, may command all from the highest even to the last; may build up Christ's household and cast down Satan's; may feed the sheep and drive away the wolves; may instruct and exhort the teachable; may accuse, rebuke, and subdue the rebellious and stubborn; may bind and loose; finally, if need be, may launch thunderbolts and lightning; *but do all things in God's Word*. (*Institutes*, IV,8,9)

Make no mistake. It's the Word, not the minister, competent to all this. Calvin stands in awe of his own calling: *divinely appointed **minister** of that Word.*

There is no hint that the minister, say John Calvin of Geneva, will peruse such a list of formidable objectives, select which one meets the needs of the hour, and then find a text to do the job! One wonders if the North American Calvinists, Puritans and Pilgrims commonly, did not fall into stratifying exposition of the Word at expense of its vitality. Perry Miller describes it in his *New England Mind.*

But not so for Calvin. Precisely the opposite of his performance.

The ossification of Calvinism. Have you noticed how rare are references to Calvin in the work of Jonathan Edwards?

For Calvin the Word has absolute priority. The moment he has decided which biblical book he will preach through, the Spirit takes command of his pulpit. As much as he chooses to cover, this is the text provided by the Spirit for the hour. What the Word here says, and here means, is the substance of his sermon and will seek incarnation in believers' behavior.

"Do all things in the Word!"

You preach! Set that Word on its oral/aural way. Let God show you the intent of his Word in the events that follow.

Imagine those Friday afternoon meetings of the preaching staff, as it became more and more obvious that, despite all shortcomings, the Word was indeed taking more and more possession of what was being made a City. And reports were coming in from around Europe, too, toward the close of Calvin's life.

Suppose, for one luscious moment, that at this time countless pulpits were ever casting the bread of the Word upon the waters of time . . . *just to see what God will do.*

At least, for now, this for the preacher: *just be brave enough to give vocalization to the Word incarnate in the Bible, text by text* — preaching what God through his Word declares and implies. Behavior will follow. Thus Cities can be created. And were.

Meaning for the congregation: *just be wise enough to demand such preaching, to will to hear and to obey, and to support him who does it, in all needs and against all agents of the Devil.* With God be the rest!

It is recorded that Paul and Silas were described in Thessalonica as "these men who have turned the world upside down have come here also" (Acts 17:6). Calvin understood that. It first got him expelled from Geneva.

Calvinist preaching was designed to offer God opportunity to achieve what his Word was inspired and competent to do. Did a gifted and courageous Trotsky, perhaps with a twinge of envy, who could equate a Calvin with a Marx as the two most revolutionary figures of the West, did he in his heart of hearts, in futile flight from the enmity of Stalin, sense the superiority of Geneva over the inferiority of his Moscow? Perhaps there is no evidence of that, but Trotsky was genius enough to share some empathy with a Calvin and his Geneva!

We know that Augustine traces "Cities" to the power of "love" — the good City to the "love of God," the evil city to the human "love of self." Calvin's "Ode" implies that no ministers, no humans, can — the matter being soberly considered — find in themselves the Power to *convert* the one "love" into the other. Only the Word is so capable. Preach it!

Calvin finds the great rhetoricians, whom he knew thoroughly enough, of little use to him, though he does promote, after Cicero, passionate speech. He knows that the results depend wholly upon the Author of the Word he proclaims. That's the essence of his "Ode."

It's always the Word. God's Word. So *ambiguously* clear.

The "Ode" embodies a clarion call to the Church. A promise of the City. But is this "Ode" likely, now, to caption homiletics sections in modern seminary catalogs, or to be displayed on framed placards gracing classroom walls?

Calvin foresaw this day coming, in the Church and her seminaries:

> Moreover, if we subdue not ourselves to the hearing of God, and suffer ourselves to be taught by him all the time of our lives, let us be afraid lest he execute the vengeance upon us, which he threatened once upon the people of Israel by his Prophet Esay [Isaiah 29:11] that his Law would be unto them as a book shut up and sealed. . . . But if we continue still in refusing the good doctrine, and become never the better for it at the year's end, as we were at the first day, at length this threat must needs light upon us, namely that we shall take the Holy Scripture into our hands, and have it preached unto us, yet we shall understand never a whit of it, though we be never so witty . . . (*Sermons*, Deut. 1:1-3).

The choice never alters: And God said . . . or . . . *Did God say . . . ?*

13. His Preaching

Can we ascertain what it was really like? Calvin's preaching in Genevan St. Peter's?

We might try in various ways, this being but one:

Take the first of twenty-two sermons on Psalm 119:

> For my own part, because I will frame myself to that manner and order which the Holy Ghost has here set down, I shall enforce myself to follow as briefly as I can the plain and true meaning of the text and without continuing in long exhortations. I will only do my best to mince or shred, as we say, the words of David, because we may the better digest them. For performance thereof I determine by the grace of God to finish eight verses apart in every sermon, and to hold myself within such compass, as that the most ignorant shall easily acknowledge and confess that I mean nothing else but to make open and plain the simple and pure substance of the text (*Sermons,* Ps. 119, 5).

He *preaches* to make "open and plain the simple and pure substance of the text." What the Book says, he wants to say, in language true to the text, true to himself.

He is fond of the metaphor of the preacher as a father at the head of the family table, breaking off and distributing pieces of bread and meat to wife and children, sometimes even "chawing" the tougher pieces for easier eating by the young.

He frequently opens a series with an "introduction." In this case, for Psalm 119:

Behold now, how the Lord our God here teaches us as it were by an ABC a most excellent song amongst the rest.

What is this "excellence"?

He summarizes in a way we can list:

1. *by which we may learn to rule and order our lives —*
2. *whereby he exhorts us to well-doing —*
3. *to comfort us in all our afflictions —*
4. *to ratify unto us the promises of salvation —*
5. *to open unto us the Gates of his everlasting Kingdom —*
6. *that we may enter into everlasting life —*

And then: "let us learn to bestow our whole endeavor and study to record the lessons which are here taught us."

". . . *[T]o record the lessons* which are here taught us" is prominent among the goals he seeks to achieve. He calls it accumulating "sound doctrine." We will come to that.

Just how will he "preach" the first eight verses of this Psalm?

Better not try a surmise.

First he reads the language with which the Psalm opens. That reveals the substance of what the Word has to *say* here. He may well be translating from the original language into French as he goes along.

Then he will turn to what the Word *means* here.

The text: *"Blessed are those which are upright in the way: and walk in the law of the Lord."*

Seems simple and plain enough.

What words will he use to "preach," that is, *incarnate in the listener* as sound doctrine, the "meaning" of David's Word here?

This is how Calvin begins:

First of all, he does us here to wit, that we understand not wherein our chief blessedness consists, and the reason is, because that we are blind, and do live in the world as savage beasts, utterly void of sense and reason: and suffer ourselves to be led and carried away of our brutish and swinish affections and lusts. And because it is so, that we are thus carried away, it is a manifest sign and token that we discern not good from evil, or else that the Devil has so bewitched us, that we think thereof no whit at all . . . and here we are to note, that David in this first verse accuses us of horrible blindness, as if he should say, Surely you are all senseless and without wit. . . . See here how mercifully our good God deals with us, who shows us how and in what manner we may be blessed and yet we for all that draw altogether backward. Does not David then of very right, justly condemn us? (*Sermons,* Ps. 119).

Is this what you expected? An approach you might have taken?

You realize that a Calvin sermon is a *Calvin* sermon. The inspired message heard for transmission by a genius, with the whole Bible at his finger-tips and the situation into which he speaks well understood. Of course, involved in this choice of meaning are the time, and the place, plus the man Calvin, all environed by God the Holy Spirit, passionately implored all the way. Together, these evoked the "substance" of what he believed God gave the text to convey. He is not "preaching" himself; he intends to be preaching the content and meaning for doctrine and behavior of this expression of the Word of God.

Would another preacher, or Calvin himself at another time, "hear" and say these words as the *meaning* of that biblical text? As to content, yes, no doubt; as to meaning, who can say?

Of one thing we can be sure: He intends his lips to be governed by what he believes to be revealed by the text, now phrased pedagogically in words of his own choosing.

Indeed, we may conclude that in Calvin's preaching all is *existential.* The *living* text encounters the *living* expositor to receive a *living* interpretation conveyed to the *living* auditor in a *lived* experience for *lived* obedience. The sermon is *lived* for preacher and for listeners. In that sense unrepeatable. His sermons could never come "out of the barrel," the nemesis of so much pulpit mal-performance. Only lectures can!

He was willing that men chosen for the task should copy what he said as preached, and that these should be passed about. But he apparently paid little attention to editing them, and judging from their chaotic history, he left little instruction regarding their preservation. The Church, like Christianity, is always in the present: "Today, if you will hear his voice. . . ." Let preacher and listener live speaking/hearing together. A Word is most a *Word* as it falls from the lips and hastens to the ear.

It seems likely that he intended the whole preaching event to be an episode in the spirit! "Going to sermon," as he tended to call it, was something of an adventure. An adventure of soul worth frequent hours in the pew for the parishioner, and long hours of study, meditation, and prayer for the preacher. All can be pristine, new, exciting. Very likely at Calvin's feet, it all was.

Casting about for an analogy, we can profit from one Everett Fox, who suggests that the great preacher is hearing, and speaking, "harmonics" of a text in a way parallel to an orchestra conductor's bringing out of a symphonic score interpretations both (1) true to the music, and yet (2) uniquely his own.

Fox poses that suggestion in his Introduction to the book *Scripture and Translation,* a collection of papers produced by Martin Buber and Franz Rosenzweig in explication of their magisterial translation of the Old Testament into German. Fox interprets their methodology by recalling a characteristic of the celebrated orchestral conductor Arturo Toscanini, known for his "literalism," that is, for insisting upon an almost slavish submission to the musical score, parallel to Calvin's awe of the biblical text.

Fox writes of Toscanini: "He saw himself as the dutiful servant of the composer and the score, yet in the very act of trying to keep his own personality out of his interpretations, he injected an element that was immediately identifiable and highly individualistic" (xxvii). So we may find it in Calvin's preaching, handicapped as we are to subservience to copyists.

We ourselves may know comparable musical experience: Yes, *that* orchestral rendition was Toscanini, or *that* was von Karajan, or *that* was Bernstein — and still, all three were, say, derived from Beethoven! Three Beethovens, then? No, one score. Just three expressions precisely in their own ways *obedient* to those musical notations. With the consequence of listening experiences inexplicably illustrating Carlyle's rejection of a "foolish consistency." Certainly relative to the preparation, the background, the vision, the courage of the pulpiteer, and to the state of mind and soul brought to the experience by the parishioner.

Calvin's preaching declines to fall into the rhetorical categories established by the classic tradition, those culminating in the *Institutes* of Quintilian. He did not think that it should.

All we can be sure of is that Calvin's intention here was the incarnation in the life and self of the believer of the dynamic reality revealed by David's Spirit-inspired linguistic incarnation of the Word. And such was the intention of every preacher desiring to be in Calvin's tradition. How widely the inspired Word was flung abroad, to create the world of the West!

Reflect that we don't know *how* the verbal command, "Let there be light . . ." actually became Light. But we can know, given faith sufficient, *that* so it was. And, though we cannot explain *how* Geneva emerged, we can observe that Calvin's tireless and extensive preaching did implant a Word which (or Who) made Geneva into the kind of City that Troeltsch describes. One which John Knox of Scotland, who lived there several years to save his life from Queen Mary, called "the veriest school of Christ." And that such preaching did incarnate the inspired Word in countless congregations, innumerable Cities, across the West for some centuries. *That it happened* can be common knowledge. We can know it, too. But *how* is ever mysterious. In the case of John Calvin, the Word preached ushered into existence the *City* of Geneva, and in the world of the West what Augustine foresaw as Cities of God.

In countless Calvinist churches, there were renditions, as it were, of the Holy Scriptures, each its own uniquely living occurrence, and still all invading history with the same living *doctrine* drawn from the same living Word of the living God to become incarnate in living human behavior.

The greatness of the West is historically verifiable.

What creative Power other than the Word scattered like the sower's seed from Calvin's and associate pulpits could possibly have accounted for that? Is there any Marxist competitor? Anything out of the Renaissance, out of the Enlightenment, out of classical tradition, anything even in Toynbee's elaborate *Cities of Destiny* to match it? Anything, that is, other than Calvinist Cities sprung up in Scotland, in England, New England — among the Dutch, who gain Lewis Mumford's approval in his *City in History* — so creative, so God-aware and therefore, so people-oriented, so sensitive to the common good, so progressively *democratic?* So like Calvin's view of civil government? Precisely built along the lines sketched in those *Institutes!* He had foreseen it; he had promoted it. There it has existence. Model to history.

"It was through the sermon," historian Perry Miller says, in his meticulous account of early America, "that nine out of ten of the elect caught the first hint of their vocation, and by continued listening to good preaching they made their calling sure. . . . when God chose to manifest Himself to a people, He came to them under the guise of ministerial eloquence" (*Seventeenth Century,* 297-98).

The ever normative principle: **Do all things . . . !**

And behold, the City!

Some Auxiliaries

13-A. Good Doctrine

We may profitably observe three facets of Calvin's preaching style, each contributing to his pulpit impact:

1. good doctrine
2. paradox
3. the absolute

Note, to begin with, that Calvin's sermons are interlarded with admonitions to "remember," to "keep in mind," and the like. All such admonitions focus upon the accumulation of an enduring store of what he frequently refers to as "good" or "sound" *doctrine.*

He says, "When we read the Word of God, when we come to sermon, we do it not to any other end and purpose, but to be instructed in good doctrine, that is to say in doctrine as is profitable to our salvation" (*Sermons,* Titus 1:1-4). Note the pragmatic equivalence between "good" and "profitable."

Good doctrine, which, in addition to pulpit proclamation may be profiled in confessions, in catechisms, and in quiet reflections, finds origin and life in sober reading and sound preaching of God's Word, and seeks incarnation in behavior. Good doctrine, then, serves as auxiliary between Word preached to, and Word enfleshed in the life of the obedient believer. "Good doctrine" functions as an elbow between the vertical of revelation preached and the horizontal of revelation obeyed. Each sermon making explanation and application of the biblical text enlarges the believer's central doctrinal deposit, which gives backbone, guide, and impetus to City-building behavior.

Good doctrine, true, that is, to inspired Scriptures, comes to form a maturing core for the believer at once disciplinary, reminiscent, inspiring, accumulated under the guidance of God the Holy Spirit from *his* Scriptures preached, read, and, most of all, obeyed.

The centrality of "sound doctrine" unites the otherwise disparate 66 books of the Bible from which Calvin so determinedly preaches. He is ever expositing complementary facets of one revelation. Karl Barth can say: "Calvin knows only **one** kingdom, that of God; only **one** truth, that of God; and only **one** goal, the glory of God. He is thus at odds with all other kingdoms, truths, or goals" (111-12).

Calvin's own summation of "sound doctrine" appears in his Genevan Catechism of 1541:

Q. *What is the chief end of man?*
And the answer: "To know God."

Q. *What is the true and right knowledge of God?*
A. When he is so known that due honor is paid to him.

Q. *What is the method of honoring him truly?*
A. To place our whole confidence in him; to study to serve him during our whole life by obeying his will; to call upon him in all our necessities, seeking salvation and every good thing that can be desired in him; lastly, to acknowledge him both with heart and lips, as the sole Author of all blessings (*Tracts and Treatises,* II, 37-38).

Here the vast variety of Holy Scripture unites as one guide to all the varieties of the obedient life.

If we are tempted, now, to assess "good doctrine" as the central theme in the thought of Calvin, we have to reckon with German theologian Hermann Bauke who argues persuasively in his *Die Probleme der Theologie Calvins* that no one has ever successfully demonstrated that one central theme affords a key to Calvin's highly complex thought, or what, if so, that key might be.

But Karl Barth runs the risk, following the *Catechism* already quoted, by writing:

Luther's heart concern was with the basis of works and not the will for them, with fighting *against* papist works and not fighting *for* works of the Spirit and love, remarkable and vital though what he said these might be. . . . To see what it looks like when a theologian really stresses and unites both parts, when the fight *for* works of the Spirit is also self-evident and a heart's concern, we may turn in comparison to the beginning of Calvin's Geneva Catechism. In the closest connection we find here the question of the chief end of human life and the knowledge of God as this end. For God created us and put us in the world in order to be glorified by us. Since he is the origin of our life, it is right that we should place this life in the service of his glory. That this should take place is our supreme good. Should it not, we are in sorrier state than animals. Nothing worse can happen to us than not living our lives for God. And here again we have true knowledge of God in which we know him as we come to awareness of the honor we owe him. But the way in which to pay this honor that we owe is fourfold: (1) by putting our whole trust in him, (2) by seeking to serve him with our whole lives and doing his will, (3) by calling upon him in need and seeking salvation and every good thing in him, and finally (4) by recognizing him with heart and mouth as the 'sole author' of all good. These four points are the basis of Calvin's whole presentation of Christianity (*Theology*, 76-77).

Barth does not, nor did Calvin, mean "good theology," the "frigid" language of the schools that, Calvin says, distances the Word from the people. Calvin writes:

Christ hath therefore been appointed by the Father, not to rule, after the manner of princes by the force of arms, and by surrounding Himself with external defenses, to make Himself an object of terror to His people; but His whole authority consists in doctrine, in the preaching of which He wishes to be sought and acknowledged (*Commentaries,* Isa. 49:2).

Again, "good" as applicable to such doctrine "as is profitable to our salvation." Calvin also says:

> Again St. Paul shows us, that it is not enough to preach the Law of God, and the promises, and what else soever is contained in the Holy Scripture, as though a man should teach in a school: but we must *Improve, threaten, and exhort.* As if he said, if we leave it to men's choice to follow what is taught them, they will never move one foot. Therefore the doctrine of itself can profit nothing at all unless it be confirmed by exhortations, and by threats, unless there be spurs to prick men withal. . . . But yet notwithstanding, that measure may be used, St. Paul adds forthwith, that it must be with doctrine: as if he said, when we exhort, we must stand upon good reason: for otherwise we should build in the air. So then doctrine is (as it were) the groundwork, and then, threatenings, and exhortations, and all the rest, is to go on with the building. . . . Moreover, let us mark in general, that the right way to awake us, is to cite us to the judgment of God (*Sermons,* 2 Tim. 4:1-2).

And again Calvin says:

> For he (Christ) is always a teacher, he is the head of the Church, yea and the only head, not to be as an idol, but to rule us with doctrine (*Sermons,* Deut. 18:16-20).

It is as doctrine that the Word is featured in catechetical teaching. It is as doctrine that the Word goes home with the parishioner from sermon, dwells in mind and heart, is food for meditation, motivates and evaluates conduct, and can be amended and enlarged and impressed both by the Scripture and by the life of obedience that good doctrine generates.

Once more Calvin says:

> S. Paul pronounceth here, that if we read the Law of God diligently, and seek in wisdom of spirit that, that is contained in it, it shall serve us for a good instruction, to bring us to faith, as also we see by experience: For whence did our Lord Jesus Christ and his Apostles draw their doctrine, but out of Moses? And if we well consider all, we shall find that the Gospel is but a simple expounding of that which Moses preached before. True it is that there is a darkness in the shadows and figures of the Law, and that God was not so gracious unto the fathers as to us: Yet so it is, that the substance of the Gospel is drawn from thence, and we have the same faith that they had, which lived before the coming of our Lord Jesus Christ. Let us therefore at this day profit in the Law of God, and let us not lose such a treasure, and let us not suffer these villains and shameful creatures to turn us aside from it, and rob us of it. I have showed already how we must learn to be faithful by the Law, to wit, by knowing this covenant which God hath made with men of his own free mercy (*Sermons,* 1 Tim. 1:5-7).

We must take note that Calvin spurns the substitution of the idea of *theology* for that of *doctrine* as key to knowing God, referring to it derisively as "divinity," by which an elite seeks to discriminate itself from the commonality. How deep and treacherous the delusion, for Calvin, of foolishly seeking to *substitute* the talking, the lecturing, the speculating, the cultivation of thought by discussion for substantive, obedient (does the Bible ever lavish praise upon learned chatter in polysyllables or foreign tongues?) existential acts that incarnate the Word.

Calvin says of such theology:

> And so it came to pass in Papistry, for there also every man changed his kind of speech, in so much that the Holy Scripture is as it were a strange language, which men call Divinity, not as doc-

trine common to all God's children, but as a craft or science for a few only. For what is true divinity? That which our Lord would have common to all his children, both to small and great, as it is expressly put down in the Prophet Isaiah; our Lord Jesus confirms it in the sixth of John. That to be faithful, and of the flock of the Church, we must be taught of God. So then when the world gave itself to such a language, that it left the Holy Scriptures, and had a clean new and strange speech, what a confusion was there in all things and a disorderous state! Yet not so far forth that the whole doctrine was directly contrary. For indeed there are some things amongst the Popish divines which are not utterly false. I say some things . . . which are of themselves not utterly false; notwithstanding, Paul condemns them in this place. And why so? For they seem to be as sorcerers, which had a kind of speech by themselves, and make I know not what conjurations. Hereby we see what is meant by these words, *Teach no other ways* [than] the naked simplicity of the Gospel . . . he warns all such as seek to get credit by vainglory, as fantastical brains are moved that way, which think that they shall not purchase sufficient commendation if they preach the Gospel purely, and therefore build and forge new speculations, and broach foolish and fantastical toys, full of vanity and leasing, and yet are they the welcomest men in the world; and when they see that their foolish devices are taken in good part, they put forth themselves more boldly, and set better leg than before. Therefore Saint Paul warns such kind of persons to surcease and leave off, and wills that we give no ear unto them, and that we suffer them not to come and make their hotchpotchs amongst us to blind our eyes in such sort, that we cannot know the true speech and language of the Holy Gospel. And this is in sum that, that is taught here (*Sermons,* 1 Tim. 1:3-4).

Again:

Why is the Gospel preached to us daily? To the end that we should be drawn away from the pollutions of the world, and be dedicated to God. Seeing it is so, let us not seek an affected kind of teaching, such as the heathen philosophy is: let us consider that God has set his mark in the Holy Scriptures. We know that the true touchstone whereby to try the goodness of any doctrine, is the referring of all things unto faith (as S. Paul says thereof), and to the glorifying of God, that men be taught to put their whole trust in the grace of our Lord Jesus Christ, to mislike themselves and to be assured of their own doings, and to frame themselves to a true amendment. Thus is it a true trial of good doctrine, when we see the preacher endeavor that God may be purely honored and served, and the praise of all power, wisdom and righteousness be yielded unto him. That doctrine is always good, and that is an infallible rule (*Sermons,* Deut. 18:21-22).

But make no mistake:

And let us not be like unto them which think that God says nothing to us in all the whole Scripture, but do this, or do that, for then this were a very thin and feeble doctrine. For if God were there as a Philosopher, to preach unto us of virtues, and to declare unto us that we must be thus governed, we should have but a pitiful cold pull of it; and because we are altogether and wholly contrary to the righteousness of God, it is impossible but that we should be grieved and troubled with whatsoever shall be said to us. But I have already showed, that the principal matter which God declares unto us in his Word is this, that he protests how well he loves us in alluring us to himself, to the end that we should not doubt, but that he will be our father in all and through all, and that we should be bold to come before him, that when there is any question of our salvation, and of whatsoever else we have need of, we should not doubt but that he is ready to hear all our prayers, that his hand is always liberally bent, to the end to give whatsoever we want. When we shall once know this to be true, then, as I have already said, the word of God shall be pleasant to us (*Sermons,* Ps. 119:113-120).

Beware:

For we must not judge of the doctrine that is set before us according to our own wit and fancy. Therefore two things need to be
matched here together. The one is, that we fully determine to be
ready to obey God, concluding in ourselves that our maker ought
to have sovereignty over us, and that we ought to be subject to
him. This is the preparation that must be made aforehand. And
afterward we must enter into judgment, that is to say, we must examine the doctrine, howbeit not with pride, nor with an opinion
that we be wise enough of ourselves, but with praying unto God
to govern us with his Holy Spirit, that we may follow the doctrine
which he shall have vouchsafed us and do our duty. This is the
doctrine which is contained in Holy Scripture (*Sermons,* 2 Tim.
3:16-17).

Barth suggests that Calvin would confess, speaking of preacher and
listener alike:

We know that we are the refuse and offscouring of the world. Before God we may boast only of his unmerited mercy and before
our fellows only of our weakness. But doctrine is very different. It
stands sublime and invincible over all the world's power and
glory, for it is not ours but that of the living God and his Christ,
whom the Father has installed as king. Christ rules, however, by
holding the whole earth in terror, notwithstanding all the power
of its iron and bronze and the splendor of its silver and gold, simply by the "rod of his mouth" (Isa. 11:4) . . . the doctrine of faith,
making us so small and God so great that precisely in this way it
sets us in the peace of sure expectation of salvation and eternal
life (*Theology,* 106-7).

Good doctrine is instrumental, never an end in itself. God is *known,*
not by head alone but in every act of obedience to the divine will as revealed in the Bible and received in transit as doctrine. Calvin himself says:

Here, David does not only declare that the word of God instructs us more perfectly than all the Sciences in the world are able to do, but also scorns the use, experience and subtlety of all whatsoever that may any way come from men, saying it is all nothing in respect of this wisdom which we learn in the school of God (*Sermons*, Ps. 119:97-104).

This, then, is the elbow, the fulcrum, the transition-point from divine Command to believing obedience: *good doctrine, the immediate goal of the sermon!*

13-B. Paradox

Few can be more easily quoted against Calvin than Calvin himself. His enemies in the tradition of sixteenth-century Bolsec contrive endless self-contradictions. A late-twentieth-century student, William Bouwsma, seems to delight in it occasionally.

As example, time and again Calvin stresses God's inestimable love for us, while in the background he has said, about this very God, as we have already heard (and it cost him no end of trouble, which changed his mind not one whit):

> We call predestination God's eternal decree, by which he compacted with himself what he willed to become of each man. For all are not created in equal condition; rather eternal life is foreordained for some, eternal damnation for others. Therefore, as any man has been created to one or the other of these ends, we speak of him as predestined to life or to death (*Institutes,* IV.21.5).

This, say, on the one hand. And, then, this on the other:

> So then, let us thoroughly consider this doctrine. . . . And since it is said that *God so loved the world that he spared not his only begotten Son, but delivered him to death for us,* (John 3:16), it is meet that I look to that. For it is very needful that Jesus Christ should pluck me out from that condemnation wherein I am. Since it is so, that

the love and goodness of God is declared unto the world, in that his Son Christ Jesus suffered death, I must appropriate the same to myself that I may know that it is to me, that God has spoken, that he would that I should take the possession of such a grace and therein to rejoice me (*Sermons,* Ps. 119:49-56).

Again, Calvin also says:

For when we shall read that God revealed himself to Abraham, and that he did help him in such a necessity, let this be our conclusion: Very well, that which God did unto his servant Abraham is to assure us that he will do the like for us, and therefore we must even now run to God for refuge and succor. See how all the testimonies which God has left unto us in the Holy Scripture of all his wonderful works, ought to serve every one of us for aids and helps (*Sermons,* Ps. 119:49-56).

Calvin fears no paradox. His preaching lives comfortably in an environment of practical paradox.

Calvin can be quoted as writing, "As I abhor paradox, I readily repudiate the saying that the treachery of Judas is as properly the work of God as the calling of Paul" (*Trent,* VI). The paradox he has in view is one that attributes human fault to God as absolute Sovereign. He abhors any effort to attribute human sinfulness to God; impossible. But the "paradox" he repudiates, say, *ontologically,* his own use of the Scripture clearly involves, *existentially,* paradox in practical form fundamental to the Christian life.

Indeed, biblical paradox divides doctrine from theology. And in practice, Calvin subscribes to, and lives effectively enough in, ultimate and ineluctable biblical paradox, the paradox of God and history, of divine omnipotence and human contingency, of divine sovereignty and human responsibility. His is a recognition of paradox that effects the neutralization of contradiction without refuge in dialectic, the escape for Hegel and Marx. Calvin navigates paradox so naturally and effortlessly, as to avoid what otherwise invalidates all attempts to systematize theology and make theoretical resolutions of its problems. However much seminary catalogs may advertise it, "systematic theology," thanks to the reality of biblical paradox, is an oxymoron. The Word of God declines ossification by the lifeless dictates of Reason, which is why Calvin thinks in terms of "doctrine" rather than "theology."

What is paradox? The term roots in the Greek notion of counterspeech. It implies the enunciation of both sides of the *contradictory* as equally true; say in the affirmation of divine sovereignty as absolute and of human responsibility as no less absolute. To affirm the truth of both components of the absolutely contradictory, without escape into evasions like "apparently contradictory" or "the contrary" in its stead, is the practical assertion of paradox. Marx, like Hegel, fled from it into the dialectic. Calvin pays no mind to the logical hiatus implied.

Paradox draws a line between sermon and treatise as forms for the Word's access to history. At issue is not preference but practice. The true sermon grapples with history, while theology simply lines library shelves, provides professors pleasant living for "chirping sweetly in the shade," and does nothing to stem the expansion of cults, cultists, and purveyors of "cheap grace." Which is why a proliferation of seminaries guarantees no constructive impact of Christianity upon history unless these produce, as did Calvin's Academy and, ultimately, his University of Geneva, fully qualified preachers, unimpressed by paradox because governed by God, not Reason, as (we've noticed) Lev Shestov never tires of stressing in works like his *Athens and Jerusalem.* The same obeisance to Reason, he says, which sent Socrates to the hemlock need not master those who find freedom in God. Calvin never bowed, in his pulpit, to the dictates of contradiction, nor did he permit these to cripple the power of the Word.

Paradox — Marx, after Hegel, chose the dialectic to avoid its icy chill, though he discriminates his form from that of the Philosopher. Calvin paid it no mind because his interest was practice, not theory nor speculation.

Essayist William Poundstone explores in his *Labyrinth of Reason,* which he subtitles *Paradox, Puzzles, and the Frailty of Knowledge,* the long historical ramifications of paradox, which we oversimplify here.

But for our purposes the term does imply the tension established in Christianity between divine sovereignty and human responsibility, both of crucial import for human behavior.

Biblical paradox is overcome only in practice, as it is everywhere in Calvin's preaching.

GOD: over, in, above, around, and behind all creation in time, with the Bible his revelation, the Word his "scepter," the pulpit his tribune, the sermon his bill of fare, the Church the communion of his saints bearing pulpits on their shoulders, and history his making through his creation. This indubitable reality on the one hand. So revealed, so witnessed to internally by the Spirit supported by conscience, so certified by experience. How blessed to know, and to *feel* (Calvin is fond of the term!) that all is God, and we in him!

MAN: On the other hand, there (as in Calvinist conventicles everywhere), seated before him on their stools in Geneva's St. Peter's, Calvin confronts divine Image-bearers, called to govern their wills by the divine Word that he proclaims, and held divinely accountable for obedient response. God rules absolutely, yes; but these are free, oh yes, free absolutely. So free in God, in Christ, and in Calvary, as to be *responsible* in life, in judgment, for obedience or rebellion. And it is to this responsibility that the sermon is addressed. *Paradox transcended* is the presumption of the sermon, of ultimate judgment, of practical freedom.

For Calvin, as already noted, *justification restores privilege to choice.* Christ can ask, because he has made choice possible.

Because Calvary liberates all, the Cross lays heavy responsibility upon all, especially upon those who dare claim it. The implication is clear and unmistakable: deny self and follow, that is obey, the Christ!

In the inexplicable symbiosis of divine and human wills, Calvin sees God as absolutely sovereign, so that the Psalmist, for instance, can recount the history of Israel as the doing of God (Ps. 97, for example), and Calvin sees humans as absolutely responsible, each so absolutely free that the risen Lord can write to everyone by way of his letter to the Church of Thyatira, "I will give to each of you as your works deserve" (Rev. 2:23). This is an inexorable moral equation enforced, Calvin holds, by the Scriptures — freedom absolute and responsibility absolute. In practice, to know that both are the way they are, and to *let neither cripple the other:* this is Calvinism, to be lived, not rationalized.

Karl Barth can write:

> In Calvin, as we see from his sermons, even the proclamation of grace wears a moral garb. This is what we have to hear and understand and take to heart and believe. For Calvin divine service was a parade ground on which imperatives held sway in every relation. . . . Without the severity of "Thou shalt" there would never have been a Reformation nor will there ever be again (*Theology,* 122).

A thought-provoking antithesis, in these times of disappearing moral restraints, and one that transcends paradox in its stride.

Barth adds:

> Calvin's severity was also linked — and this is the main point — to the great saving or destroying either-or that hung like the sword of Damocles over humanity and over every individual, and that for him resulted directly from the knowledge of God, a thought whose critical significance he felt like no other reformer, and perhaps like no one at all until we come to Kierkegaard, in whom we find the same severity. May I remind you again of the opening of the Geneva Catechism, which tells us expressly that those who do not glorify God in their lives have sunk to the level of the beasts (123).

The choice is ever the same, between the "trousered ape," however elegantly garbed and suavely behaved, time-bound and self-enslaved, and the *New Man* accessible through faith in Christ Jesus, he whose passion and death sufficed to expiate the sin of the world and liberate from bondage those who hear, bondage also to Reason. The choice between these two life-styles Calvin sees as that severe sword hanging over every human being every hour. Long ago Moses said it, in language never altered: "See, I have set before you this day life and good, death and evil. If you obey the commandments of the LORD your God which I command you this day, by loving the LORD your God, by walking in his ways, and by keeping his commandments and his statutes and his ordinances, then you shall live and multiply . . . therefore choose life . . ." (Deut. 30:15-16, 19).

To choose, however theoretically impossible, however camouflaged, however distorted by the Lie, is, *paradoxically,* what Calvin knows that living implies, every moment, be it in hovel or in palace.

And Barth, with a sly grin, says: "Those who live with smaller views of a smaller cause than Calvin's really find it much easier to be less severe than he was" (125). Might he be thinking of the likes of those whom Schleiermacher called "the cultured despisers" of Christianity, who find childlike belief beneath them, and thus paradox insurmountable?

Calvin, like Marx, grasps his role as that of a social engineer; he, unlike Marx, was in the service of a transcendental order, indeed of the Master of history himself. So Trotsky saw them. But, unlike Marx (who knew the Bible well enough) and more like Quixote, Calvin sees the Sword of the Spirit, sheathed in the Holy Scripture, as the weapon against sin and deception provided humankind by the living God, and as a scepter brandished upon the lips ordained to the purpose in accord with the revelation of the Lord from whose mouth "issued a sharp two-edged sword" (Rev. 1:16). The Word illumines the path, and empowers its following, thus making humanity *(1) freed at Calvary and thus, (2) wholly responsible in a world (3) entirely God's!* With judgment awaiting us all.

Marx develops his powerful, rational ideology as deliberate substitute for revelation, as antidote to biblical paradox, and thus invites into time all that revelation condemns — tyranny, theft, torture, and murder. Precisely in this context, Marx tries to sanctify rebellion as, in the words of Albert Camus' powerfully insightful tract, *The Rebel,* "replacing the reign of grace by the reign of justice" (56) — a brilliant profile of twentieth-century dynamics, and an almost incidentally (though Jean-Paul Sartre caught it — did Camus?) insightful perception of the fundamental contrast of Marxism and Christianity, the two most revolutionary drives in the West. "How to live without grace and without justice" now tortures the contemporary world, Camus concludes, observing that "the will to power has taken the place of the will to justice" — and become a "frenzy . . . which is called power" (225). Camus' book led to the legendary break between Sartre and him, two underground Resistance comrades. Surprisingly, Camus' percipient tract does not fulfill the promise of its own premises and reduces the reader merely to whistling while passing the cemetery of human rationalist aspirations. Camus fails to acknowledge the *paradoxical* route of Christian faith to the goal of justice, which his powerful essay surely implies.

Thus, while Bunyan's "Christian" sensed no paradox and only passed through cities, as do now the itinerant evangelists, en route to the heavenly mansions, Calvinists built or redid their Cities along the way, while Marxists made the Gulag a symbol of the un-community fathered by paradox in command. Barth writes that while Luther "puts the *German Theology* side by side with the Bible and Augustine, Calvin called it twaddle the devil had produced to confuse the simple gospel and said that it was deadly poison for the church" (84). Calvin would no doubt have found the sentiments of *Theologica Germanica* paralleled in *Pilgrim's Progress,* both of them as strikingly innocent of grappling with or passing by paradox as is today's crusadist evangelism, and therefore as constructively ineffectual. Bunyon's classic built no Cities, fused no revolts, individualizing the Pilgrim whose familial responsibilities were only an afterthought, into the egocentric figure typical of those "saved" in religious crusades.

Weathering paradox, and absorbing the critical jibes which so-doing entails, is as indispensable to preaching in Calvin's style today as in his own time. The Kingdom may be enforced and discipleship lived in defiance of the mandates of Reason.

Beware!

On the Calvinist pulpit the inspired Word excludes the "law" of excluded middle. Duty has no place to hide.

13-C. The Absolute

Christianity is preeminently the religion of Word, which (or Whom), as already noted, Calvin defines as "the everlasting Wisdom, residing with God from which all oracles and prophecies go forth" (*Institutes*, I,13,6).

For Calvin, the obedient pulpit rises high above all other sources of guidance in providing platform for the proclamation of "a certainty wherein we may not fail," guaranteed in the inspired language restlessly alive within the covers of Holy Scripture.

Calvinism implies total obedience to the Word incarnate in the biblical text, whatever its linguistic embodiment. It implies absolute confidence in the Way of the Word as divine Agent. And so, let the Word be spoken and exposited, leaving the rest to God.

Philosopher John Dewey writes of *The Quest for Certainty,* so characteristic of human nature, sought in so many ways through many means, none ever absolute. But John Calvin finds certainty, absolute and irrefutable, in one Source, the Word of God, revealed by grace within the covers of the Bible — a surety not as Calvin's own attainment, but a discovery as divine gift of Faith. That discrimination is most important. Assurance is gift, not achievement.

Where can we turn for unqualified certainty amidst the rush of events, the confusion of tongues, the clamor of experts, the vicissitudes of life? To put that question is to fashion context for its answer. Nowhere in all the creation is absolute certainty provided by the created. (The reader will note the *paradox:* It is absolutely certain that there are no natural absolute certainties!) For absolute certainty we must — and thanks to Christ, we can — turn outside the realm of space and time, to the one point where the Eternal intersects them, often called "today" in biblical parlance. Of such intersection, Calvin has no doubt. We must tune to the Voice of the Trumpet heard from afar and echoed from off the pulpit. A certain Voice. The Lord's Voice in human tongue. The Word of God preached!

On whose Word besides the Lord's could we totally and absolutely rely? And how could a Word be God's without entailing absolute certainty? Amidst the bibble-babble of endless religious chatter, of competing authorities, with experts and expertise inundating the avenues of communication, flooding unasked upon the soul, chatter endlessly multiplied, rapidly becoming pervasive via the Internet, there is but one Word affording us "a certainty wherein we may not fail," as Calvin says in preaching on Job 10. And to its promulgation but one institution qualified from above, the Church of Jesus Christ. And but one kind of lips authorized to do the promulgating — those lips authorized by ordination in the Church. And in that Church the symbol of divine preference, the pulpit raised above those who sit thus at the feet of their Lord. "By this means, and by this means only, . . ." as put by Cromwell.

And how shall we *know* that the biblical Word is God's, and how be sure that we hear aright? Only, Calvin holds, by the internal witness of God the Holy Spirit, who confers an assurance none other can provide nor corrode.

> Calvinism sought to renew the whole of Christianity, in doctrine and the Church, in ethics and in dogma, solely through the Bible. Its greater reforming radicalism was due to this fact, and to the active character of its religion, which was based on the doctrine of election (Troeltsch, II, 587).

The Word preached derives from that Word incarnate in the inspired Book, the Holy Scriptures.

For Calvin, Bible and Word are synonymous, preaching and Word are inevitably correlative.

Let this be a firm principle: No other word is to be held as the Word of God, and given place as such in the church, than what is contained first in the Law and the Prophets, then in the writings of the apostles; and the only authorized way of teaching in the church is by the prescription and standard of his Word (*Institutes*, IV,8,8).

Calvin is certain: *"no other word . . . !"* A certainty not won, but given by God the Holy Spirit.

Nor are we required to certify for ourselves the right of Scripture to speak with authority:

St. Paul here flatly shows us that if we will do homage to God, and be subject to him, we must receive what is contained in the Law and Prophets. And because no man might give himself liberty to choose what he would, and so obey God in part, he says that the whole Scripture has this majesty, whereof he speaks, and that it is all profitable. To be short, Paul pronounces here that men must not take lumps and morsels of it such as they like best, and what they fancy out of the Holy Scripture, but they must conclude without exception, seeing that God has spoken in his Law and his Prophets, we must wholly and only cleave fast and stick to it. And thus we see what St. Paul's meaning is in this place. . . .

A man might ask the question, seeing there is such an uprightness in the Law and the Prophets, to what purpose serves the Gospel, then? For it seems that St. Paul's doctrine itself is needless to us. This is easy to be answered, that the Gospel was not given to man to add anything either to the Law or the Prophets. Let us read and turn over all the leaves of the New Testament, we shall not find one syllable added either to the Law or the Prophets; it is but only a plainer setting forth of that which was taught before (*Sermons*, 2 Tim. 3:16-17).

How tempting, as Calvin saw right well, to stress, say, the biblical offer of salvation while slighting the biblical account of creation; how easy to focus on the promises while neglecting the admonitions, taking "lumps and morsels of the Book such as men like best," on Omar Khayyam's principle, "take the cash and let the credit go."

But, such a theft is forbidden by the Word thus plundered. For Calvin the Bible comes all or none, perhaps prophetic in the seamless robe worn by Jesus, which the soldiers declined to violate (John 19:23). The effort to have it otherwise, in times like our own, only vitiates the Word altogether and negates its authority. How could Natural Man, at odds with God and bereft of hope except on God's terms, prescribe how God will reveal himself, or what kind of behavior constitutes that "knowing" which is the goal of life?

Nor can it be *demonstrated* that the Bible *is* God's Word. Nor "proved" that the Book there at your hand *is* or *is not* divine revelation. What one could prove, another could disprove. All is of faith, and faith a work of God as by the Spirit through the Word listened to, confirmed in obedience to it. Calvin takes no refuge in the virtues of the so-called "autographa," the now lost original manuscripts, as safe lodging for faith in an infallible Word. The Bible he knows, believes, and strives to obey is the one there on your own night stand.

The equation of great genius with childlike simplicity, so characteristic of Calvin, who can hold his own intellectually with the greatest theologians given the Church, is never more on display than in his attitude toward the Scriptures. Sufficiently competent in the original biblical languages to make his own translation of such caliber as to influence the development of modern French (compare Jacques Pannier, *Calvin écrivain*), as Luther had done for German, Calvin declines to join the contest to *prove* or *dis*prove the reliability and authority of Scripture. What, indeed, might "prove" mean in this context? For Calvin it is always just Faith, endowed by the Holy Spirit, which *recognizes* in the Bible an absolute authority, precisely as requisite to preaching with complete confidence, and, still more, as indispensable to living the salvation that is the obedient life. Such faith is discovery, not construct, received, not made.

We can perceive, then, that the Bible **must**, for Calvin, be inspired, that is, be "Spirit-breathed," if the sermon is to proclaim the Word that (or Who) creates the City. The most persuasive ground for expectation of Spirit-inspired biblical infallibility is desperate human need of it. We *need* anchorage, stable footing in the flow of time, authentic guidance unto salvation, met precisely in its own terms by the overflowing love of God. By whatever metaphors this necessity is expressed — anchor against the storm, rock in the wilderness, serenity amidst turmoil, Light upon life's way — the thrust is ever the same: God alone can through the Word "breathed" by the Spirit make "faith unambiguous forever," as Calvin puts it in the *Institutes* (I,6,2). Because God is; because God loves; because faith is fundamental to salvation as guide and motivation to obedience, the Word that undergirds faith must come in absolute reliability — *and does!*

All in God's dealing with us is proportional to our need. Biblical infallibility is not his whim, but our necessity. For Calvin, one only satisfied not by our demonstration, not by our resolution of all problems involved in believing the Bible trustworthy, but on the witness of the inspiring Spirit in mind and soul that the Word God brought to expression speaks true. Though this goes far beyond our understanding of how that can be so, a conviction confirmed, not by our "scholarship," but in every act of obedience.

"What will happen," he queries, "to miserable consciences seeking firm assurance of eternal life if all promises of it consist in and depend solely upon the judgment of men? Will they cease to vacillate and tremble when they receive such an answer? Again, to what mockeries of the impious is our faith subjected, into what suspicion has it fallen among all men, if we believe that it has a precarious authority dependent solely upon the good pleasure of men!" (*Institutes,* I,7,1).

This is, surely, precisely the predicament of so-called modern man, of the "modern man" of all ages, of all arrogance, all "science," all self-reliance, plagued on every hand by unresolved uncertainties over the fundamentals of existence, our loudest asseverations only witnessing the fragility of our convictions.

The Word is divine gift. The human language that incarnates it to become the Holy Scripture is itself of the divine largesse. The goal of divine Love in providing us an inspired and therefore infallible Word is unmistakable: *"For by his Word,"* as we have already noted, *"God rendered faith unambiguous forever, a faith that should be superior to all opinion"* (*Institutes,* I,6,2).

Calvin is well aware of the Socratic distinction that philosophers drew between "knowledge," or certainty, and "opinion," sufficient for its purpose but not always trustworthy. Scripture affords us knowledge of a most unique kind, from God, authenticated by God, utterly reliable, conveyed through the Word incarnate in the Scriptures. That this doctrine generated countless controversies Calvin well knew. That faith which holds the Bible true is neither created in these disputations, nor sustained by them, nor defeated thus Calvin also knew.

> Hence the Scriptures obtain full authority among believers only when men regard them as having sprung from heaven, as if there the living words of God were heard (*Institutes,* I,7,1).

Is this the boast of a propagandist, seeking to beguile the gullible? No, it is the mature judgment of a theologian as learned and as gifted as any of those given by the Lord to his Church, a man whom unbelief in any of its myriad forms — ancient or modern — could not daunt for an instant. Modernity, flaunting its "scientific" accomplishments, would not awe him but only arouse his scorn. *What now, little man?!* How well he was aware that cynicism, skepticism, arrogance — however clothed — are of old time, all forms of the ancient temptation, "Did God say . . . ?" (Gen. 3:1).

Calvin occupies and helps define the turning point at which history became modernity. He was given to discern in the biblical Word a Power available to humans competent to close much of the gap between the ancient vision of the City and its near-realization in the West. It was he who effectively formulated the sermonic technique for clothing that Word with historical Power. He wrote:

> Well, then, if faith depends upon God's Word alone, if it applies to it and reposes in it alone, what place is now left for the word of the whole world? And anyone who well knows what faith is can-

not be in doubt here. For faith ought to be upheld with such firmness as to stand unconquered and unwavering against Satan and all the devices of hell, and the whole world. We shall find this firmness solely in God's Word. Then here is a universal rule that we ought to heed: God deprives men of the capacity to put forth new doctrine in order that he alone may be our schoolmaster in spiritual doctrine as he alone is true who can neither lie nor deceive. This pertains as much to the whole church as to individual believers (*Institutes*, IV,8,9).

Calvin declines the academic ploy that separates the Word from the Bible, and he declines the subtle deviation that dissolves the text into an "interpretation" formed by each reader or listener, one's as valid (or invalid) as another's.

The Word intersects time through providing encounter with the Eternal God. What Hegel remarks on in his *Phenomenology* as the ever elusive "Now," gone even as the term is pronounced, slipping through our fingers while attended to, becomes "today" when the Speech of God is heard as divine address, the occasion of opportunity. So it was for Abraham, Calvin noted, and so for us. The voice of the preacher stops time in its flight, to recognize our "now" as God's "today" in which God provides us the messenger and his sermon. There the Word establishes the "moment," to use Kierkegaard's metaphor, which validates the "leap of faith," given substance and definition by whatever Word of revelation is said, heard, and incarnated in the act.

"In the beginning was the Word . . ."

"And God said . . ."

Between these two resides the awesome mystery of divine communication vehicled by Word, so effectively put to social, historical consequence from the pulpit of Geneva's St. Peter's and its innumerable offspring as the Light and Power calculated to populate the West with Cities.

Not only yesterday, but no less tomorrow.

And of Results

14. Work Is Worship

With an eye on City-building, we should take note of one substantive, democratizing facet of Calvin's pulpitry, his stress upon work as worship. Not in the church, but on the job!

Cities are built by, and flourish upon, daily work. Marx knew that, said that, and exploited its reality. So did Adam Smith. Both were preceded in so doing by Calvin.

He dwells on the necessity of work, the worship in work, whenever the text in hand provides occasion. He knows that civilization is the creation of work of all kinds, done by people of all kinds, offering *meaning* to their living because they are, deliberately or otherwise, giving themselves to the City.

André Biéler devotes a brilliant, substantial, and highly instructive volume to the role of work in Calvin's thought, preaching, and behavior in his substantial *La pensée économique et sociale de Calvin.* He meticulously exposits Calvin's influential role in the economic life of Geneva and of the West.

Much of the Christian life is, after all, exercised in what is the "worship" done in daily obedience, commonly on the job. For Calvin and Calvinists, the factory, the kitchen, the counting-house, the business office — these and their like in countless forms may be perceived as sanctuaries where God is daily honored by labor for which he provides life, talent, time, and opportunity, repaid by the words, "Well done, good and faithful servant . . ." (Matt. 25:21).

"For when a man takes pains for his living, he serves God" (*Sermons*, 1 Tim. 4).

"Let each of us remember," Calvin writes, "that he has been created by God for the purpose of laboring, and of being vigorously employed in his work, and that not only for a limited time, but till death itself, and what is more, that he should not only live, but die, to God" (*Commentaries*, Luke 17:7).

For Calvinism, an index of the constructive occupations in any society is guide to forms of divine worship practiced there, consciously or unconsciously forms of serving God through self-denial for promotion of the common good.

Preaching on St. Paul's admonition, "Let the thief no longer steal, but rather let him labor, doing honest work with his hands, so that he may be able to give to those in need" (Eph. 4:28), Calvin says,

> Let us consider for a moment how many occupations there are in the world which serve for nothing but corruption, and to rake in money, as they say. It is true that men are not aware of it. And why? Because all men are contented that such as have plenty should be prodigal, in order that their money may be scattered among all. Again, such as cannot get their living otherwise (as they see it), are inventing new devices every day to pick fools' purses and of such as are addicted to thoughtlessness.... Accordingly, St. Paul has drawn a distinction here. For it is not enough for a man to say, "Oh, I labor, I have my craft, or I have such a trade." That is not enough. But we must see whether it is good and profitable for the common good, and whether his neighbors may fare the better for it.... And for this reason we are likened to members of a common body.... God must go before us, as if he called us to Himself, and we follow the way He shows us by His Word. Surely He will only approve of occupations which are profitable and serviceable to the whole community, and which reflect good also to all men.... When a man comes to consider by what trade his son may best earn his living and provide for himself and his family after marriage, at the same time let him also

see to it that he serves his neighbors, and that the use of his skill and occupation may redound to the common profit of all men (*Sermons,* Eph. 4:28).

Of those whose choice of occupation fails the criterion of the common good, Calvin warns, "You may say, I have worked hard at this or that. Indeed! But you have served the devil. For just as the devil has his martyrs, so he also has his servants" (*Sermons,* Eph. 4:28).

Consider the consequence for a healthy civic life of such sermonizing as this: "For a woman to take pains about housewifery, to make clean her children in their dress, to kill fleas, and such like, although this be a thing despised, yea and such that many will not vouchsafe to look upon, yet are they sacrifices which God accepts and receives, as if they were things of great price and honorable. Therefore let women study this lesson day and night, that first of all they play the housewives" (*Sermons,* 1 Tim. 2).

The all-seeing glance of God penetrates job-obscurity, of women and men alike, young or old, workplace monotony, total public indifference and contempt, to profile a job in any form of "socially useful" labor as an opportunity to serve him, as if by "things of great price and honorable." How direct an address to labor dissatisfaction everywhere. It promises far more creative resolution of "class struggle" than the Marxist solution of violent revolution, or the intellectuals' solution through the psychology of conflict-resolution, or the on-going practice of unionization and various forms of state welfarism.

God's Word holds exploitation, whether of employer or of employee, up to judgment. The Calvinist/Puritan "work ethic," as Max Weber came to describe it, contributed in major ways to the great constructive impact that Christianity had upon the Cities of the West. And indeed a powerfully preached Word through Calvinism could in this day contribute to the solution of labor problems often unresolved in strike and threat, and dissatisfactions festering where the all-seeing glance of God is unknown or ignored. Calvin's perception ranges deeper and more broadly than even the medieval attempts to define and achieve "just wage" and "fair price."

Recall Calvin's alternative, in his letter to Sadoleto, to a "Christianity" perverted into an easy route to heaven: "It is not a very sound theology to confine a man's thoughts so much to himself, and not to set before him, as the prime motive of his existence, zeal to illustrate the glory of God. For we are born first of all for God, and not for ourselves.... This zeal ought to exceed all thought and care for our own advantage.... It certainly is the part of the Christian man to ascend higher than merely to seek and secure the salvation of his own soul" (*Reformation Debate*, 58).

And it is here, also, that through our choice a religious appreciation of reality, as in Calvin, and a presumably "scientific" analysis of reality, as in Marx, part ways.

God is worshiped on the job because in daily working we make ourselves useful to others, and therefore to divine ends. A perception widely promoted off the Calvinist pulpit.

"City" implies space in time and place for the countless acts of self-giving called "love," many simply in forms of daily work, which together create civilization and culture. Art galleries house but lifeless copies of the living works of art who are growing up everywhere under the auspices of the City, forms of life chaperoned by good civil government.

Consider the irony that millions of dollars may change hands over, say, possession of Rembrandt's painting of his son Titus, while ignored and often abused are flesh and blood Tituses entrusted by God to the care of the City. Calvin sees civil structure designed by God to environ, say, the artistic development of each one of his Image-bearers. Was not a Rembrandt given to teach that there is a potential artistry implicit in the very existence of children of the City awaiting awakening by the touch of a divinely guided hand of love? Rembrandt wanted to defer the ravages of time by painting his child in more enduring stuff than the human body naturally provides. Calvin perceived the City as given to prepare lives enduring into eternity through effort expended in obedience to divine Law.

"Most influential," says historian Sydney Ahlstrom of the social impact of Calvinist/Puritanism, "was the new emphasis on serving the Lord in one's vocation — as tradesman, as merchant, as an artisan, or as a magistrate or 'citizen' . . . a 'this worldly asceticism,' in Max Weber's famous phrase . . ." (118).

Let labor take note, and the pulpit claim its attention: "It will be no small alleviation of his cares, labors, troubles and other burdens, when a man knows that in all these things he has God for his guide. The magistrate will execute his office with greater pleasure; the father of a family will confine himself to his duty with more satisfaction; and all, in their respective spheres of life, will bear and surmount the inconveniences, cares, disappointments, and anxieties which befall them, when they shall be persuaded that every individual has his burden laid upon him by God. . . . There will be no employment so mean and sordid — provided we follow our calling *(vocationi)* — as not to appear truly respectable, and be deemed highly important in the sight of God" *(Institutes,* III,10,6).

Adam Smith celebrates in his *Wealth of Nations* the "cunning of history" in providing that work done for self-interest correlatively serves the common good. But consider the brilliant Light bursting upon the awful workday monotony that threatens to poison the passage of irretrievable time implied in a preaching that elevates labor to status of divine worship. This is true on the assembly line, at the workbench, in the melee of the stock market, indeed in whatever the occupation.

If God accepts — *indeed, if it is God* who accepts — then of course such work of whatever type becomes "of great price and honorable." How else could it be? Reflect on it. Let it be preached. Major taproot of a City! In Calvin's time, yes, and now no less! Unequaled resolution of "labor problems." What other observers despise, indeed what those who are themselves involved despise, when understood as in fact blessed with divine approval undergoes a "transvaluation of values" unrecognized by Nietzsche.

Muse on the consequence if thousands of pulpits were relentlessly proclaiming divine approbation, as service and worship, of daily labor of all kinds, the approval, not of the elite, not of the wealthy, not of the sophisticated, not of the learned, not even by way of the pay check, but of God upon the regimen of the daily grind?!

Calvin preached, "So then let women learn to rejoice when they do their duty, and though the world despise it, let this comfort sweeten all toil they may have that way, and say, 'God sees me, and his Angels, who are sufficient witnesses of my doings, though the world do not allow of them'" (*Sermons,* 1 Tim. 2). And, indeed, not women only, but everyone who constructively labors!

Jesus Christ sacrificed himself, Paul says, to obtain a people zealous for good work(s). Such a people, Calvinism shows, build the City.

In his famous *Protestant Ethic and the Spirit of Capitalism,* Max Weber contrasts for spiritual "flavor" the conclusion of (Calvinist) Milton's *Paradise Lost* with that of (Catholic) Dante's *Divine Comedy.* Dante, he says, "stands speechless in his passive contemplation of the secrets of God," while in Milton, "One feels at once that this powerful expression of the Puritan's serious attention to this world, his acceptance of his life in the world as a task, could not possibly have come from the pen of a mediaeval writer. But it is just as uncongenial to Lutheranism, as expressed for instance in Luther's and Paul Gerhardt's chorales" (87-88).

Calvin said, "There is then an inseparable bond between God's grace and the doctrine of the good life" (*Sermons,* Titus 2).

Ernst Troeltsch wrote:

Since for him [Calvin] the central point of religion is not the blessedness of the creature, but the Glory of God, so also the glorification of God in action is the real test of individual personal reality in religion. In Calvin's view the individual is not satisfied with mere repose in his own happiness, or perhaps in giving himself to others in loving personal service; further, he is not satisfied with an attitude of mere passive endurance and toleration of the world in which he lives, without entering fully into its life. He feels that, on the contrary, the whole meaning of life consists precisely in entering into these circumstances, and, while inwardly rising above them, in shaping them into an expression of the Divine Will. In conflict and in labor the individual takes up the task of the sanctification of the world, always with the certainty, however, that he will not lose himself in the life of the world; for indeed in everything the individual is only working out the meaning of election, which indeed consists in being strengthened to perform actions of this kind (II, 588).

God is "known" to the Calvinist on the job because God is served in work, even when done ostensibly only for secular ends. And the consequence is that the secular is nowhere better served, while kept in its place of subordination to the spiritual. And in this unique combination lay the City-building power divinely characteristic of Calvinism/Puritanism and its sermonizing.

So the Word preached reaches down into the shadows of the City, into its ghettos and most poverty-stricken wards, to *touch with meaning* the work done there. And the Word similarly touches with significance work done anywhere in seeming absence of meaning, be that in ghetto or soaring skyscraper. *God sees. God knows. God records for ultimate recompense!* What a revolution such an appreciation of daily labor could again effect in the Western world, were the pulpit once more trained for and dedicated to such preaching.

Troeltsch continues:

> This peculiar combination of ideas produces a keen interest in politics, but not for the sake of the State; it produces active industry within the economic sphere, but not for the sake of wealth; it produces an eager social organization, but its aim is not material happiness; it produces unceasing labor, ever disciplining the senses, but none of this effort is for the sake of the object of all this industry. The one main controlling purpose of this ethic is to glorify God, to produce the Holy Community, to attain the salvation which in election is held up as the aim; to this one idea all the other formal peculiarities of Calvinism are subordinate (II, 607).

Writing in his *Calvin's Doctrine of the Christian Life,* Ronald Wallace paraphrases Calvin: "We must not believe the lie that the Devil tells us when he seeks to persuade us that laboring and housework are secular affairs that do not concern God. We must not separate the present mundane life from the service of God. God accepts honest and upright work as service agreeable to Himself. If the chambermaid and the manservant go about their domestic tasks offering themselves in their work as a sacrifice to God, then what they do is accepted by God as a holy and pious sacrifice pleasing in His sight" (*Sermons*, 1 Cor. 10). What Wallace translates as "sacrifice," in Calvin's language is *"une oblation saincte et pure,"* the French *"oblation"* recalling the Old Testament transition of the temporal into the eternal upon the altar of sacrifice, permitting, indeed requiring, the recognition of work as specifically a self-sacrificial act of worship. The temple altar is on the job!

It is evident that the ethical character of work is always proportional, the ratio between talents and opportunity, which God provides, and the quality of endeavor, which people provide. "Well done, good and faithful servant . . ." (Matt. 25:21, 23) was lavished no less upon the few-talented productive servant than upon the many-gifted one. One who declined to work was denounced and consigned to eternal punishment (Matt. 25:30), and one who worked only to fill barns with produce dedicated to himself was characterized as "You fool!" (Luke 12:20) — applicable no less to those who fill their minds with useless knowledge, and think their obligation to society satisfied in the production of treatises read among themselves. Status disappears in devotion, selfless devotion, assiduous exploitation of the creation as commanded in the beginning: "subdue" (Gen. 1:28) the earth.

Is this, then, in contradiction to the Lord's admonition, "Do not labor for the food which perishes, but for the food which endures to eternal life, which the Son of man will give to you" (John 6:27)?

No, the dominical admonition is correlative to the right appreciation of daily work as satisfying simultaneously both temporal and eternal concerns. Intrinsic to the life of obedient use of talent and opportunity by way of constructive labor is its sculpting the soul of the laborer through working in God's vineyard, the world of stuff put to hand by Providence.

Ever promoted by the pulpit, good work(s) became the hallmark of Puritanism/Calvinism, and the foundation of the enormous achievements in City-making characteristic of the West. The purpose, sobriety, self-discipline requisite to good work, and endowed upon history by Christianity, have brought humankind closer than ever before to realizing the enduring vision of the true City. This vision, so betrayed by Communism, glitters still on the horizon of a dawning century if Calvin's path be perceived, understood, and followed. The Light upon such a path and the Power to follow that Light reside in the Word, most effective as preached!

Calvinism aimed consciously and systematically at the creation of a Holy Community. It co-ordinated the activity of the individual and of the community into a conscious and systematic form. And since the Church could not be fully constituted without the help of the political and economic service of the secular community, it was urged that all callings ought to be ordered, purified, and enkindled as means for attaining the ends of the Holy Community. Thus the ideal was now no longer one of surrender to a static vocational system, directed by Providence, but the free use of vocational work as the method of realizing the purpose of the Holy Community. The varied secular callings do not simply constitute the existing framework within which brotherly love is exercised and faith is preserved, but they are means to be handled with freedom, through whose thoughtful and wise use love becomes possible and faith a real thing. . . . This kind of asceticism produced, as an important by-product, that ideal of hard work, of the prosecution of work for its own sake, as a duty in itself, which is anything but a natural habit of mind, and which can only be understood in the light of a religious energy which can thoroughly transform the natural instinctive life. Once this psychological state of mind has been created, it can then, through a process of metamorphosis of purpose, be detached from its original meaning and placed at the disposal of other ideas; in various ways this process often takes place at the present day. It is, however, precisely at this point that we can observe the difference between nations which had been educated on Catholic, Lutheran, or Calvinist lines. To people who have been educated on Calvinistic principles the lazy habit of living on inherited income seems a downright sin; to follow a calling which has no definite end and which yields no material profit seems a foolish waste of time and energy, and failure to make full use of chances of gaining material profit seems like indifference to God. From the Calvinist point of view laziness is the most dangerous vice; it is hurtful to the soul from the standpoint of ascetic discipline, and harmful to the community from the standpoint of social utilitarianism (Troeltsch, II, 611).

Calvin was not the first, it must be observed, to see work as in itself uniquely the worship of God. St. Benedict (sixth century A.D.) had coined the famous phrase *laborare est orare (to work is to pray)* for his monks. But that subtle perception did not, on the whole, infect the outlook of the clerical hierarchy which chose to live like civil potentates thinking this befitting as retainers of the King of Kings, nor did it spread to the laity by whom Cities are made.

Moreover, Calvin teaches that Christian duty has far wider scope than one's own vocation: "For it is not enough for us to abstain from hurting and grieving of our neighbor. Neither is it enough for us to go about to discharge us of our duties. But when we see any man unjustly trodden down, and a good cause go to wrack, we ought to oppose ourselves against every such wicked act and injury, and as it were to take part with God, who as he is the commender of all equity, so will he also have us to maintain it forasmuch as we are his children" (*Sermons,* Ps. 119:121-128). Of course the Calvinist is a social activist. As on God's *mission* in ways not usually associated with that idea!

Calvin and the Calvinist recognize the Church as radical, oriented by its Message to the roots of personal and social behavior. Unlike so-called contemporary Liberation Theology, however, shot through as it is with Marxism, Calvinism found dynamic in the Word, not in ideology. Christianity, in Calvinist form, finds that the Bible authentically preached makes creative social revolutionaries while ideology makes only rebels. So Calvin experienced it; so Calvin came to promote it.

The goal of the Church as it developed under Calvin's hand in Geneva became the temporal realization of *Christianopolis* (the term is from Lewis Mumford). It is also to achieving this *temporal* end that the Christ donned human flesh, lived, died, and rose again to reign from heaven. It is toward this *penultimate* that the risen Lord commissions his pulpit ministry to labor until the Age of the Ultimate dawns by way of the tomb and Last Judgment.

Indeed, from Calvin's perspective, with *ultimate* human destiny predetermined by God's election/reprobation, why else find Christianity and the Church in history at all, than for the spiritualization of the temporal *pen*-ultimate (a term meaningful to Bonhoeffer in his desperate struggles with Nazism) in the realization of the City in time and place?

15. Mother of Cities:
Glimpse of the Record

Calvin and Calvinists aimed at creation of the City. And widely succeeded.

Were there, then, "Cities" fetched into existence by Calvinist preaching? Or almost-Cities, at least? Where Pericles and those who gave substance to his anticipations might well have felt at home?

Oh yes, both "Cities" and countries that grew up around them. Indeed there has grown up a vast literature on the democratic achievement, sponsored by Calvinist Puritanism, that is becoming the civilization of the Western world. We can take a peek or two:

GENEVA: First of all, Calvin's own Geneva. We have heard encomiums and characterizations that praise and describe the "miracle of Geneva" in ecstatic terms. Long before his relatively early death, John Calvin had acquired a track record, and Geneva drew throughout the century men and women of unusual character and talent, attracted by the vision of participation in a true City growing up in the shadow of the Alps. A memorial account of the story, notable among many of such histories, can be found in *La vie ardente du premier refuge français, 1532-1602*, by F. Fournier-Marcigny, the book itself an ardent advocate.

SCOTLAND: In Calvin's own century, John Knox and colleagues brought to fruition in Scotland a nation shaped by Calvinist pulpits to be a people uniquely their own version of the Genevan impetus. Citizens these were who became known for their integrity, strength of character, stubborn courage in matters religious, and determination to be themselves in obedience to the Word.

FRANCE: Akin indeed to these Scots were the French Huguenots who in the same century so flourished as indictment of the iniquities of France as to provoke their own massacre on the St. Bartholomew's eve of 1572.

CROMWELL'S ENGLAND: Thomas Carlyle awakened England and the world to the significance of Oliver Cromwell (1599-1658), various biographers lauding this Calvinist's achievements in his relatively brief reign as Lord Protector, 1653-1658. In his *God's Englishman,* left-leaning Christopher Hill credits Cromwell's regime with establishing English sea power and extension of sound foreign relations, providing at home greater democracy than ever before and some time after, liberating social and religious behavior, and providing for economic prosperity including the poor. Lady Antonia Fraser clothes both Cromwell and his attainments in promotion of the New Era in felicitous terms in her *The Lord Protector.*

Philosopher David Hume, writing in his *History of England* of the period of Cromwell, said, "So absolute was the authority of the crown, that the precious spark of liberty had been kindled, and was preserved, by the *Puritans* alone; and it was to this sect that the English owe the whole freedom of their constitution" (V, 134). Skeptic Hume, who awakened philosopher Kant from his "dogmatic slumber," was no disciple of Calvin's but did apprehend in Puritanism the prints of his footsteps.

THE NETHERLANDS: Dutch Prince William of Orange-Nassau, called William the Silent (1533-1584), leads the liberation of the Netherlands out from under much of the yoke of Spain toward the end of Calvin's century. One of the authorities on this period, James Lathrop Motley, so describes him in his youth: "He was disposed for an easy, joyous, luxurious, princely life. Banquets, masquerades, tournaments, the chase, interspersed with the routine of official duties, civil and military, seemed likely to fill out his life. His hospitality, like his fortune, was almost regal" (I, 257).

But the One who mastered John Calvin had his crucible for this follower of Calvin also. Awakened by Luther, Motley says, and then mastered by Calvin, "Without a particle of cant or fanaticism, [William] had become a deeply religious man. Hitherto he had been only a man of the world and a statesman, but from this time forth he began calmly to rely upon God's providence in all the emergencies of his eventful life. . . . He writes, 'I see well enough that I am destined to pass this life in misery and labor, with which I am well content, since it thus pleases the Omnipotent, for I know that I have merited still greater chastisement. I only implore Him graciously to send me strength to endure with patience'" (I, 257; II, 265).

Before being cut down by an assassin's bullet, the Calvinist Prince had led to liberation seventeen of the twenty-seven Dutch provinces by overcoming humanly insurmountable odds. Motley thus describes the fruits of the Prince's life and labor: "From the hand-breadth of territory called the province of Holland rises a power which wages eighty years' warfare with the most potent empire on earth, becoming itself a mighty state, and binding about its own slender form a zone of the richest possessions of earth, from pole to tropic, finally dictates its decrees to the empire of Charles [the Fifth]" (I, iii). Calvinism at work!

Harvard historian and art critic Simon Schama evokes in his brilliant study of the seventeenth-century Calvinist Netherlands, *The Embarrassment of Riches,* a highly perceptive portrait of the spirit and content of that Calvinist-inspired national "City." As illustrative:

> Imagine a twelve-year-old Dutch boy, apt, decently Christian. . . . Every Sunday (at least) a cascade of rhetoric would crash down from the pulpit, invoking the destiny of the Hebrews as though the congregation were itself a tribe of Israel. Lines dividing history from Scripture dissolved as the meaning of Dutch independence and power was attributed to the selection of a new people to be a light unto the nations. In this Netherlandish addendum to the Old Testament, the United Provinces featured as the new Zion, Philip II as a king of Assyria and William the Silent as a godly captain of Judah. The boy was to understand that he was a Child of Israel, one of the *nederkinderen,* dwelling under the protection of the Almighty for so long as he heeded His commandments. The nation to which he belonged had been delivered from bondage and raised up to prosperity and might through the

power of the covenant made with the Lord. Were it to stray from the paths of righteousness it could expect to be humbled as Israel and Judah had been humbled before it. As the boy grew to manhood, his conduct should exemplify acceptance of this covenant, and, accordingly, blessing would be showered upon him. To a great extent this scriptural exhortation was the common idiom of all Calvinist and Puritan cultures of the early seventeenth century (93-94).

About the Netherlands we read, "Travelers repeatedly chorused their amazement at being able to walk the streets at night unmolested or with the sure knowledge that if they were set upon the felon would be quickly apprehended. They were equally astonished at the absence of the tribes of beggars that populated most European cities" (Schama, 583).

NEW ENGLAND: While across the sea in New England Calvinist/ Puritan adherents of the Genevan model satisfied one historian's description as typical of many: "It is safe to assume, then, that the influence of puritanism, in the broad Calvinistic sense, was a major force in the late colonial period, and that it contributed uniquely and profoundly to the making of the American mind when the American mind was in the making. . . . It was not surprising that patriotism was preached from the pulpits, and that political agitators would have drawn their inspiration from puritan ministers" (Perry, 359).

A first-hand account appears in Cotton Mather's *Magnalia Christi Americana (Great Works of Christ in America)*. In the "Attestation" he contributed to Mather's work, Pastor John Higginson writes:

It has been deservedly esteemed one of the great and wonderful works of God in this *last age,* that the Lord stirred up the spirits of so many thousands of his servants, to leave the *pleasant land* of England, the land of their *nativity,* and to transport themselves, and families, over the *ocean sea,* into a *desert land* in America, at the distance of a *thousand leagues* from their own country; and this, merely on the account of *pure and undefiled Religion,* not knowing how they should have their *daily bread,* but trusting in God for *that,* in the way of *seeking first the kingdom of God, and the righteousness thereof*... giving an example of true *Reformed religion* in the *faith* and *order* of the Gospel; according to their best light from the *words* of God... [dated Salem, the 25th of the first month, 1697] (Mather, I, 13).

Mather himself describes the colonizing intent thus: "'Tis now time for me to tell my reader, that in our age there has been another essay made not by the French, but by British Protestants, to fill a certain country in America with Reformed Churches; nothing in doctrine, little in discipline, different from that of Geneva" (I, 40).

The lineaments of the true City, which still democratize, energize, and embolden the Western world, take their hue from the colors of mind, soul, and spirit laid upon Cities made in the spirit of John Calvin through pulpits loyally proclaiming the Lordship of Christ after the model of Geneva. The stubborn resistance of the West to both Marxist and Fascist domination owes its energies and strength to echoes of the Word spread abroad by Calvinist pulpits now catastrophically grown timid and confused.

Yes, there were Calvinist-inspired Cities and countries grown up around them. Calvin did become, in Spengler's terms, a "world power," all by the preaching of God's Word. Also in Sweden, in Poland, in Eastern Europe, with kings and princes in correspondence with Calvin's Geneva.

The historical record is. Our recounting might be much expanded. The Word which enlivened it is.

The world waits now upon ambassadors appointed in the mold of Calvin to continue preaching Cities not only into existence but no less into growing excellence. To that, the alternative is chaos and death. On the right choice the world hangs, as it were, trembling in the balance.

Do all things in the Word!

Select Bibliography

Adoratskii, Vladimir Viktorovich, ed. *Karl Marx and Frederick Engels: Selected Correspondence, 1846-1895.* Trans. Dona Torr. New York: International, 1942.

Ahlstrom, Sydney. *Religious History of the American People.* New Haven: Yale University Press, 1972.

Augustine, Saint. *The City of God.* Trans. Marcus Dods. New York: Modern Library, 1950.

Balke, Willem. *Calvin and the Anabaptist Radicals.* Trans. W. Heynen. Grand Rapids: Eerdmans, 1981.

Barth, Karl. *The Doctrine of the Word of God: Prolegomena to Church Dogmatics,* Vol. I, 1. Trans. G. W. Bromiley. Edinburgh: T&T Clark, 1975.

———. *The Theology of John Calvin.* Trans. G. W. Bromiley. Grand Rapids: Eerdmans, 1995.

Battles, Ford Lewis. *Analysis of the Institutes of the Christian Religion of John Calvin.* Grand Rapids: Baker, 1980.

———. *Interpreting John Calvin.* Grand Rapids: Baker, 1996.

Bauke, Hermann. *Die Probleme der Theologie Calvins.* Leipzig: Hinrichs, 1922.

Bercovitch, Sacvan. *Puritan Origins of the American Self.* New Haven: Yale University Press, 1975.

Berger, Heinrich. *Calvins Geschichtsauffassung.* Zurich: Zwingli-Verlag, 1955.

Beza, Theodor de. "A Short Life of John Calvin." In *Tracts and Treatises*, Vol. 1 by John Calvin. Trans. H. Beveridge. Grand Rapids: Eerdmans, 1958.

Biéler, André. *Calvin, prophète de l'ère industrielle: Fondements et methode de l'ethique calvinienne de la société.* Geneva: Labor et Fides, 1964.

————. *La pensée économique et sociale de Calvin.* Geneva: Librairie de l'université, 1959.

Bohatec, Josef. *Budé und Calvin.* Graz: Bohlaus, 1950.

————. *Calvin's Lehre von Staat und Kirche.* Breslau: M. & H. Marcus, 1937.

Boisset, Jean. *Sagasse et saintete dans la pensee de Jean Calvin.* Paris: Presses Universitaires de France, 1959.

Bonhoeffer, Dietrich. *The Cost of Discipleship.* Trans. R. H. Fuller. London: SCM, 1959.

Bouwsma, W. J. *John Calvin: A Sixteenth-Century Portrait.* New York: Oxford University Press, 1988.

Breen, Quirinus. *John Calvin: A Study in French Humanism.* Grand Rapids: Eerdmans, 1931.

Brook, Benjamin. *Lives of the Puritans.* London: J. Black, 1813.

Cadier, Jean. *The Man God Mastered: A Brief Biography of John Calvin.* Trans. O. R. Johnston. Grand Rapids: Eerdmans, 1960.

Calvin, John. *Calvin's Commentary on Seneca's De Clementia.* Trans. F. L. Battles and A. M. Hugo. Leiden: Brill, 1969.

————. "Catechism of the Church of Geneva." In Vol. 2 of *Tracts and Treatises: With a Short Life of John Calvin by Theodore Beza,* 3 vols. Trans. H. Beveridge. Grand Rapids: Eerdmans, 1958.

————. *Commentaries.* Ed. D. W. Torrance and T. F. Torrance. 45 vols. Grand Rapids: Eerdmans, 1948-57.

————. *Golden Booklet of the True Christian Life: A Modern Translation from the French and the Latin.* Ed. H. J. van Andel. Grand Rapids: Baker, 1952.

————. *Institutes of the Christian Religion.* Ed. J. T. McNeill. Trans. F. L. Battles. 2 vols. Philadelphia: Westminster, 1960.

————. *Johannes Calvins Lebenswerk in seinen Briefen.* Ed. R. Schwarz. 3 vols. Neukirchen-Vluyn: Neukirchener, 1961.

————. *Letters of Calvin.* Ed. J. Bonnet. 4 vols. Edinburgh: Constable, 1855-58.

————. *New Testament Commentaries.* Ed. D. W. Torrance and T. F. Torrance. 12 vols. Grand Rapids: Eerdmans, 1963-74.

————. *A Reformation Debate: Sadoleto's Letter to the Genevans and Calvin's Reply.* New York: Harper, 1966.

————. *Sermons on Deuteronomy.* Edinburgh: Banner of Truth, 1991.

————. *Sermons on Ephesians.* Edinburgh: Banner of Truth, 1981.

————. *Sermons on Galatians.* Edinburgh: Banner of Truth, 1997.

————. *Sermons on Job.* Edinburgh: Banner of Truth, 1993.

————. *Sermons on Psalm 119.* Audubon, N.J.: Old Paths Publications, 1996.

————. *Sermons on 2nd Samuel.* Edinburgh: Banner of Truth, 1992.

————. *Sermons on Timothy and Titus.* Edinburgh: Banner of Truth, 1984.

————. *Tracts and Treatises: With a Short Life of John Calvin by Theodore Beza,* 3 vols. Trans. H. Beveridge. Grand Rapids: Eerdmans, 1958.

Camus, Albert. *The Rebel.* Trans. A. Bower. New York: Knopf, 1956.

Carlyle, Thomas. "Oliver Cromwell's Letters and Speeches." In *The Works of Thomas Carlyle (Complete).* 13 vols. New York: P. F. Collier, 1987.

Castrén, Olavi. *Die Bibeldeutung Calvins.* Helsinki: Suomalainen Tiede-akatemie, 1946.

Catton, Bruce, and William B. Catton. *The Bold and Magnificent Dream: America's Founding Years, 1492-1815.* Garden City: Doubleday, 1978.

Cole, Henry, trans. *Calvin's Calvinism.* Derbyshire: Sovereign Grace Union, 1927.

Davies, Rupert E. *The Problem of Authority in the Continental Reformers: A Study in Luther, Zwingli, and Calvin.* London: Epworth Press, 1946.

Dewey, John. *The Quest for Certainty: A Study of the Relation of Knowledge and Action.* New York: Minton, Balch, 1929.

Doumerge, Émile. *Jean Calvin: les hommes et les choses de son temps.* 7 vols. Lausanne: G. Bridel, 1899-1927.

Dowey, Edward A., Jr. *The Knowledge of God in Calvin's Theology.* New York: Columbia University Press, 1952.

Favre-Dorsaz, André. *Calvin et Loyola: Deux réformes.* Paris: Presses Universitaires de France, 1948.

Foster, Herbert D. *Collected Papers of Herbert D. Foster, Professor of History at Dartmouth College, 1893-1927.* [New York]: Priv. Print., 1929.

Fournier-Marcigny, F. *La vie ardente du premier refuge français, 1532-1602.* Geneva: Mont-Blanc, 1942.

Fox, Everett, ed. *Scripture and Translation: Martin Buber and Franz Rosenzweig.* Bloomington: Indiana University Press, 1994.

Fraser, Antonia. *Oliver Cromwell: The Lord Protector.* New York: Knopf, 1973.

Ganoczy, Alexandre. *Le jeune Calvin: Genèse et evolution de sa vocation reformatrice.* Wiesbaden: F. Steiner, 1966.

Gardiner, Samuel R. *Constitutional Documents of the Puritan Revolution, 1625-1660.* Oxford: Oxford University Press, 1889.

Graham, W. Fred. *Constructive Revolutionary: John Calvin and His Socio-economic Impact.* Richmond: John Knox, 1971.

Halaski, Karl, ed. *Der Prediger Johannes Calvin.* Neukirchen-Vluyn: Neu-kirchener, 1966.

Haller, William. *The Rise of Puritanism: Or Puritanism's Way to the New Jerusalem as Set Forth in Pulpit and Press.* New York: Harper, 1957.

Hancock, Ralph C. *Calvin and the Foundations of Modern Politics.* Ithaca: Cornell University Press, 1989.

Hegel, Georg Wilhelm Friedrich. *The Phenomenology of Mind.* Trans. J. B. Baillie. London: Allen & Unwin, 1949.

Higman, Francis. *The Style of John Calvin in His French Polemical Treatises.* London: Oxford University Press, 1967.

Hill, Christopher. *God's Englishman: Oliver Cromwell and the English Revolution.* New York: Dial, 1970.

Hume, David. *The History of England, from the Invasion of Julius Caesar to the Revolution in 1688.* New ed. 6 vols. New York: Publishers Plate Renting Printing Co., n.d.

Hunt, George L., ed. *Calvinism and the Political Order: Essays Prepared for the Woodrow Wilson Lectureship of the National Presbyterian Center, Washington, D.C.* Philadelphia: Westminster, 1965.

Kevan, Ernest F. *The Grace of Law: A Study in Puritan Theology.* Grand Rapids: Baker, 1965.

Kingdon, Robert M. *Geneva and the Coming of the Wars of Religion in France, 1555-63.* Geneva: Droz, 1956.

Léonard, Émile G. *Histoire générale du Protestantisme.* 3 vols. Paris: Presses Universitaires de France, 1961-64.

Leube, Hans. *Kalvinismus und Luthertum im Zeitalter der Orthodoxie.* Aalen: Scientia-Verlag, 1966.

Lowrie, Walter. *Kierkegaard.* London: Oxford University Press, 1938.

Mather, Cotton. *The Great Works of Christ in America.* 2 vols. London: Banner of Truth, 1979.

Marx, Karl. *Capital: A Critical Analysis of Capitalist Production.* 3 vols. Moscow: Foreign Languages, 1954-62.

Maxwell, William D. *The Liturgical Portions of the Genevan Service Book.* Linslade, England: Faith Press, 1965.

McGrath, Alister E. *A Life of John Calvin: A Study of the Shaping of Western Culture.* Cambridge, Mass.: Blackwell, 1990.

McKim, Donald, ed. *Readings in Calvin's Theology.* Grand Rapids: Baker, 1984.

McLoughlin, William G. *New England Dissent, 1650-1833: The Baptists and the Separation of Church and State.* 2 vols. Cambridge, Mass.: Harvard University Press, 1971.

McNeill, John T. *The History and Character of Calvinism.* New York: Oxford University Press, 1954.

Melanchthon, Philipp. *The Loci Communes.* Trans. C. L. Hill. Boston: Meador, 1944.

Menzies, Allan. *A Study of Calvin and Other Papers.* London: Macmillan, 1918.

Miller, Perry. *Errand into the Wilderness.* Cambridge, Mass.: Belknap, 1956.

————. *New England Mind: From Colony to Province.* Cambridge, Mass.: Harvard University Press, 1953.

————. *New England Mind: The Seventeenth Century.* New York: Macmillan, 1939.

Millet, Olivier. *Calvin et la dynamique de la parole: Étude de rhetorique réformée.* Paris: Honoré Champion, 1992.

Monter, E. William. *Calvin's Geneva.* New York: Wiley, 1967.

Motley, James L. *Rise of the Dutch Republic.* 3 vols. New York: McKay, n.d.

Mumford, Lewis. *The City in History: Its Origins, Its Transformations, and Its Prospects.* New York: Harcourt, Brace & World, 1961.

Neal, Daniel. *The History of the Puritan Reformation.* 2 vols. London: R. Hett, 1732.

Niesel, Wilhelm. *The Theology of Calvin.* Philadelphia: Westminster, 1956.

Nijenhuis, W. *Calvinus Oecumenicus.* 's Gravenhage: Nijhof, 1959.

Parker, T. H. L. *Calvin's Preaching.* Louisville: Westminster/John Knox, 1992.

Pannier, Jacques. *Calvin écrivain: Sa place et son rôle dans l'histoire de la langue et de la littérature française.* 2nd ed. Paris: Fischbacher, 1930.

Perry, Ralph Barton. *Puritanism and Democracy.* New York: Vanguard, 1944.

Poundstone, William. *The Labyrinth of Reason: Paradox, Puzzles, and the Frailty of Knowledge.* New York: Anchor-Doubleday, 1988.

Quervain, Alfred de. *Calvin: Sein Lehren und Kampfen.* Berlin: Furche-verlag, 1926.

Schama, Simon. *The Embarrassment of Riches: An Interpretation of Dutch Culture in the Golden Age.* New York: Knopf, 1987.

Senarclens, Jacques de. *De la vraie Église selon Jean Calvin.* Geneva: Labor et Fides, 1964.

Shestov, Lev. *Athens and Jerusalem.* Trans. Bernard Martin. Athens, Ohio: Ohio U. Press, 1966.

Smart, James D., trans. *Revolutionary Theology in the Making: Barth-Thurneysen Correspondence, 1914-1925.* Richmond, Va.: John Knox Press, 1964.

Smith, Adam. *The Wealth of Nations.* New York: Modern Library, 1936.

Smits, Luchesius. *Saint Augustin dans l'oeuvre de Calvin.* 2 vols. Assen: Van Gorcum, 1957-58.

Sohm, Walter. *Die Schule Johann Sturms und die Kirche Strassburgs in ihrem gegenseitigen Verhältnis, 1530-1581.* Munich: Oldenburg, 1912.

Southgate, Wyndham Mason. *John Jewel and the Problem of Doctrinal Authority.* Cambridge, Mass.: Harvard University Press, 1962.

Spengler, Oswald. *The Decline of the West.* Vol. 1, *Form and Actuality.* Trans. Charles Francis Atkinson. New York: Knopf, 1926.

————. *The Decline of the West.* Vol. 2, *Perspectives of World History.* Trans. Charles Francis Atkinson. New York: Knopf, 1928.

Sprenger, Paul. *Das Rätsel um die Bekehrung Calvins.* Strasbourg: Istra, 1924.

Stauffer, Richard. *The Humanness of John Calvin.* Trans. George H. Shriver. Nashville: Abingdon, 1971.

Torr, Dona, trans. *Karl Marx and Friedrich Engels: Selected Correspondence, 1846-1895.* The Marxist Library, no. 29. New York: International, 1942.

Toynbee, Arnold, with Jane Caplan. *A Study of History.* New York: Portland House, 1988.

Troeltsch, Ernst. *The Social Teaching of the Christian Churches.* Trans. Olive Wyon. 2 vols. New York: Macmillan, 1931.

Volkogonov, Dmitri Antonovich. *Lenin: A New Biography.* Trans. Harold Shukman. New York: Free Press, 1994.

Walker, Williston. *John Calvin, the Organiser of Reformed Protestantism, 1509-1564.* New York: Putnam, 1906.

Wallace, Ronald S. *Calvin's Doctrine of the Christian Life.* Grand Rapids: Eerdmans, 1959.

Walzer, Michael. *The Revolution of the Saints: A Study in the Origins of Radical Politics.* Cambridge, Mass.: Harvard University Press, 1965.

Weber, Max. *The Protestant Ethic and the Spirit of Capitalism.* Trans. Talcott Parsons. London: Allen & Unwin, 1930.

Wendel, François. *Calvin: The Origin and Development of His Religious Thought.* Trans. Philip Mairet. New York: Harper & Row, 1963.

Williams, Charles. *The Figure of Beatrice: A Study in Dante.* London: Faber & Faber, 1943.

Williams, George Huntston. *The Radical Reformation.* London: Widenfeld & Nicolson, 1946.

Wilson, David A. *Carlyle on Cromwell and Others.* London: Kegan Paul, 1925.

Witte, J. L. *Het Problem individu-gemeenschap in Calvijn's geloofsnorm.* 2 vols. Franeker: Wever, 1949.

Index

Bernard, James (Pastor), letter to, 14
Bible: authority from heaven, 110; certainty absolute, 105; comes all or nothing, 108
Bolsec, bitter enemy, 27
Bonhoeffer, Dietrich, "cheap grace," 50

Calvary, liberates all, xviii
Calvin, John: academic degrees, 27; aristocrat, 54; Barth's characterization, xiii; civic activism, 41; conversion from Catholicism, 31-32; expulsion from Geneva, 25-26, 39; counts that "early training," 39; motto on emblem, 58; returns from exile, 59; seeks advice on return, 58; *Golden Booklet of the Christian Life*, 63
Calvinist "Cities": Geneva, 126; Scotland, 126; France, 127; Cromwell's England, 127; Netherlands, 127; New England, 129
Christ: wants to rule, 21; why he came, xvii
Christianity, forms of, x
Christianopolis (Mumford), goal of Church for Calvin, 124
Church: attendance not mandatory,

70; Mother of Believers, 44; Mother of Cities, 44
Church and State, separation of absurd, xx
Christian life: foundation of 63; elements of, 67
Citizen, revolutionary term, 20
City: classic views of, xv, xvii; Calvin's view, xix; two types (Augustine), 4; Marxist, 8
Cop, Nicolas: Rector of Sorbonne 29; condemned, with Calvin, by Inquisition, 30
Cromwell, Oliver, enunciates Calvinist view of Word, 20-21
Crusade evangelism, Calvin rejects, 16

Darwinism, undermines Genesis and thus Bible, 54
Democracy, political face of religious perspective, xix
Divinity, "strange language," 93
Doctrine: Christ rules by, 92; rises sublime over all, 96; summarized in Genevan Catechism, 90

Declaration of Independence, embodies Calvinist doctrine, xix
Demonic, always the enemy, xiv

137